GOURMET FRENCH

Macarons

OVER
75

Unique
Flavors

Festive
Shapes

Mindy Cone

FRONT TABLE BOOKS

An Imprint of Cedar Fort, Inc.
Springville, Utah

© 2013 Mindy Cone

ISBN 13: 978-1-4621-1219-7

Published by Front Table Books, an imprint of Cedar Fort, Inc.
2373 W. 700 S., Springville, UT, 84663
Distributed by Cedar Fort, Inc., www.cedarfort.com

Library of Congress Cataloging-in-Publication Data on file

Cover and page design by Erica Dixon
Cover design © 2013 by Lyle Mortimer
Edited by Casey J. Winters

Printed in China

10 9 8 7 6 5 4 3 2 1

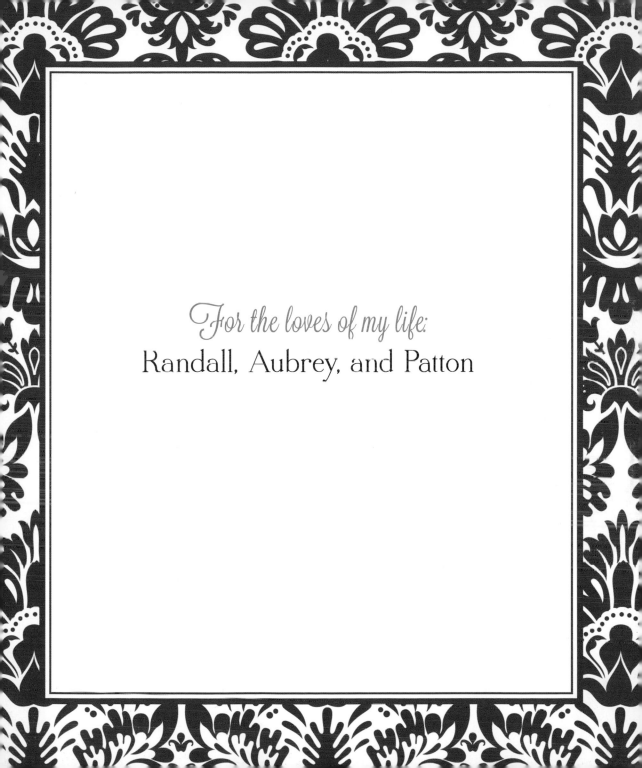

For the loves of my life:
Randall, Aubrey, and Patton

p. 14

p. 29

CONTENTS

v

p. 07

p. 62

p. 160

p. 200

p. 174

p. 128

p. 190

vii

Love at First Bite

I REMEMBER THE FIRST TIME I HAD A MACARON. Who could forget? I was curious about this unique sandwich cookie I had heard so much about and seen in every beautifully styled dessert display. As an entertainment and party blogger, I am always fascinated by party trends. So when I stumbled across them while on vacation, I just had to try one . . . or five . . . in the interest of research, of course.

It was *love* at first bite.

If you've never had a macaron, you're in for a surprise! It's quite the experience! There is a crisp thin outer shell, which gives way easily to a moist, chewy almond meringue cookie, followed by a silky center of flavorful filling. It is chewy yet soft, delicate yet flavorful, small yet satisfying! No wonder I became obsessed!

I returned home determined to locate every bakery within 100 miles that sold these wonderful cookies! With a luscious treat like this there were surely to be bakeries filled with them, right? Well, not quite. I could surely order them online then, right? Well, not for that price. Why were these amazingly mouthwatering sandwich cookies so hard to find and at such a high price?

So I made a decision. I would make them.

Macarons have a reputation for being a bit tricky. Don't let the number of ingredients fool you—those four ingredients are high maintenance! It has been quite a journey to perfecting the art of the French macaron—many recipes, types of equipment, flavors, and baking

1

temperatures and times have been tried and tested to finalize my own method. Most important, I discovered that making these is less about the recipe and more about the technique and lessons that you learn along the way. But don't worry—I'll dish all my tricks and tips to you! This book will not only guide you through the process of making a perfect macaron—in taste, texture, and appearance—but it will also open your eyes to a world of creative dessert opportunities! Who says a macaron has to be a circle? Who says you can't use sprinkles and candy melts to make them as adorable as they are tasty? Once you learn the basics for making consistently perfect, traditional macarons, the possibilities are endless in flavor and design! Using the templates provided in the accompanying CD, you are no longer confined to the conventional circular shape. You can make apples, pumpkins, ghosts, trees, flowers, animals, cupcakes, and many other shapes to fit each season, holiday, or celebration.

This beautiful, delicate, gooey, colorful sandwich cookie has captivated my attention from the first bite, and I haven't turned back—so get ready . . . you will probably be the same!

Mindy Cone

History
of a French Macaron

Is a French macaron the same thing as a macaroon?

T HE WORD *MACAROON* encompasses a variety of cookies that are coconut and meringue based. So while it is not incorrect, it is not clear to what you are referring. To help distinguish between several different desserts, most have adopted the French one "o" spelling for the popular Parisian meringue-based sandwich cookie, thus leaving the double "o" term—*macaroon*—for the gooey, shredded coconut dollop dipped in chocolate.

Macaron cookies are thought to originate from Italy but were brought to France by Catherine de' Medici in 1533, when she was married to the king of France, Henry II. The word *macaron* comes from the Italian *maccarone*, meaning "fine dough." These first macarons were simple: almond powder, sugar, and egg made into a flat, plain biscuit. Lots of tales surround those early macarons, including an interesting one involving nuns in the city of Nancy who made these flat almond cookies and sold them to make a living. They became know as *les Soeurs Macarons*—the macaron sisters—and their recipe is still found in shops of Nancy to this day!

By the mid-seventeenth century, cities across France began to adapt the basic ingredients through small variations, and recipes began to emerge in French cookbooks. It was not until the 1900s that Pierre Desfontaines (second cousin of Louis Ernest Ladurée of the renowned Parisian tea salon founded in 1862—Ladurée) had the idea of adding ganache to a shell and topping it with another to create the sandwich double-decker shape we see popular today. With this concept, Ladurée has become an icon and standard for macarons with their mouth-watering flavors and consistent, perfect, simple beauty.

SHELL

FOOT

FILLING

Anatomy
of a French Macaron

The Parisian macaron has several important features:

THE SHELL should be smooth, shiny, and flat with no peaks. It should be crisp and thin such that it gives way easily with pressure. This shell comes only through proper rest time between piping and baking—an average of 30 minutes, depending on the humidity of your kitchen.

THE FOOT (*pied*) should have a ruffled or frilled appearance that is an even and consistent size all around the macaron. This occurs during baking as the air escapes out the bottom of the cookie and lifts it up. The foot therefore is a sign of proper baking and ensures that the macaron will have the right texture—light, soft, and slightly chewy.

THE FILLING should be contained within the edge of the shells without spilling over but should be enough to be seen and separate the two shells. This is the main source of flavor for the macaron and a great opportunity to introduce additional texture as well.

5

Tools

GRAM SCALE

It may seem daunting to use, but this tool is *very* easy to use and *very* important! You can find a gram scale anywhere that sells baking tools—I found mine at my grocery store for only fifteen dollars. It is very important to be accurate when making macarons.

HAND MIXER OR STAND MIXER WITH WHISK ATTACHMENT

Both will work—it comes down to individual preference. I used my hand mixer for a long time . . . and I have the arm muscles to prove it!

SIFTER OR BOWL SIEVE

There are several reasons for sifting the dry ingredients. First, sifting will aerate the mixture and ensure the ingredients are evenly mixed. Second, sifting will remove larger almond pieces that will be discarded to ensure a smooth shell texture. I recommend sifting your dry shell ingredients two or three times. This is a particularly important step when making chocolate shells to incorporate the cocoa powder evenly.

BAKING SHEETS

Heavy aluminum baking sheets are best, but anything will do. If your sheets are particularly thin, doubling up will help protect the bottom of the macaron from browning.

PARCHMENT PAPER AND/OR SILICONE MAT

In my experience, I prefer name-brand, good-quality parchment paper. However, when I create a uniquely shaped macaron with delicate extremities or triangular points (ears, tails, and so on), I prefer a silicone mat. This way I can ensure that the details will rise evenly with the rest of the macaron during baking. Often parchment paper will stick to these smaller details and produce a footless or lopsided macaron, or worse—cause them to crack. Some chefs I have talked with recommend using both, by layering the parchment on top of a silicone mat. The reason for this is to shield the bottom of the macaron from browning—particularly if you have thin baking sheets. Whatever you decide, *do not* use aluminum foil! You will never get your macarons off them in one piece!

SPATULA

I am snobby when it comes to my spatulas! One of the most important steps of making a macaron is incorporating the dry ingredients into the meringue—this is called *macaronnage*. I look for a spatula that is flat with broad and fairly flexible (I prefer silicone) wings on both sides. But again . . . I am very picky! If you plan on making more than one color or flavored shell, use a separate spatula for each. Washing risks the possibility of introducing water or soap to the meringue, which will inhibit it.

CLEAN BOWLS

At minimum, you will need one large bowl for whisking meringues and one small bowl for dry ingredients. Avoid using a plastic bowl for whipping egg whites because they can harbor traces of grease or fat. Water, grease, and soap residue are enemies of meringues and prevent them from properly forming. So be sure your bowl is clean and dry!

PASTRY BAG AND PIPING TIPS

Unlike most cookies, macarons are piped onto a baking sheet. This requires a pastry bag and a few different tips. I use Wilton-brand featherweight or disposable pastry bags. For one recipe, I recommend a 16-inch bag, and for the half recipe, I recommend a 12-inch bag. You will need the Wilton 12 tip (¾ cm.) or 10 tip (or a comparable product) for all of your basic circular macarons as well as most of the unique shapes. Depending on the design, you may also need a smaller tip. Wilton 3, 4, or 5 will work great. Piping your macarons is an important step to ensure they bake correctly! See the section on piping tips and techniques (page 23) for more details.

Mindy Cone

OVEN THERMOMETER

This tool will ensure that your temperature reading is accurate. Temperature accuracy is particularly important when making macarons of different shapes and sizes because the oven time and temperature vary.

MAGNETS

A few small magnets will help to keep your parchment paper in place. If you are not careful when piping, the parchment paper can lift and adhere to the side of the macaron. As the cookie bakes, it rises upward off the parchment. The slightest adhesion can cause the delicate cookie to rise unevenly or crack. Using magnets to secure the parchment will minimize this issue. Leave the magnets as the shells rest, but remove them right before baking.

TOOTHPICKS

So many times I am reaching for a new toothpick! I use them when coloring my meringues, to pop air bubbles in shells, and to maneuver batter into delicate shapes. Be sure to have some of these handy!

FOOD PROCESSOR

If you prefer to make your own almond flour or if you need to grind nuts for the variation recipes, this will be a necessary tool. Grind the nuts as fine as possible to achieve a smooth shell texture. Additionally, this tool is often recommended as a way to combine your dry ingredients. When I first started making macarons, I followed this suggestion for every batch. One day I got lazy and decided to skip it. I could not tell the difference and have not used it since! Simply sifting 2 or 3 times produces the same result.

Ingredients

 HERE ARE ONLY 4 ESSENTIAL INGREDIENTS to making a French macaron shell. Here are some tips and tricks to make sure you are giving your cookies the best possible chance for success!

ALMOND FLOUR

This key ingredient is what gives the macaron shell its moist, chewy texture and nutty flavor. You can make your own or buy it from most grocery stores. If you make your own, try to get almonds that are blanched and skinless. I prefer to buy pre-ground almond flour. It may seem expensive at approximately 10 dollars per pound, but if you do the math it's not bad at all! A 1-pound bag will make about 4½ batches (about 100 sandwiched, 1½-inch macarons) which works out to less than 10 cents per cookie—quite the far cry from the bakery price tag of macarons!

POWDERED (ICING/CONFECTIONER'S) SUGAR

Nothing tricky here—any brand of powdered sugar will do.

EGG WHITES

+ FOR BEST RESULTS, use aged room-temperature egg whites.

+ TO SEPARATE YOUR EGGS, crack the egg and hold over a small bowl. Carefully separate the two shell halves, allowing the whites to fall into the bowl as you transfer the yolk from one half to the other. If *any* yolk gets into the whites, then you need to start over with a clean bowl and new egg whites because fats in the yolk will interfere with the formation of a meringue.

+ TO AGE YOUR EGGS, I recommend letting them sit at least 24 hours at room temperature covered by a cheesecloth or paper towel. This will allow the eggs to slightly dehydrate and produce a much stronger meringue. A full recipe calls for 100g of aged egg whites. If you are using large eggs, this is approximately 4 egg whites for a single batch and 7 egg whites for a double batch. Be sure you are measuring the 100g after you have aged them.

SUPERFINE SUGAR

This is regular granulated sugar that has been ground down into smaller crystals. It is also know as caster sugar or baker's sugar. The finer crystals dissolve faster and result in a lighter texture. While it is readily available at most grocery stores, you can make your own by grinding granulated sugar in your food processer for a minute or two.

CREAM OF TARTAR

Not all macaron recipes call for this, but I prefer it as an insurance policy for my meringue! The mild acid helps the meringue to form and stay stable.

FOOD COLORING

One of the most beautiful things about macarons are their colors! From soft pastels to the bright and bold, it is important to understand how to color your macarons without hindering the final product. There are three main coloring systems: liquid, gel, and powder. As you read earlier, excess water will inhibit a meringue from forming or maintaining shape. Liquid and gel dye contain water. Thus, the best food coloring system is powdered dye. Since this is a dry ingredient, it is sifted in with the powdered sugar and almond flour. However, powdered dyes are less common and slightly more difficult to track down. The next best option is gel dye since it will have lower water content than liquid dye. Both of these are added to the meringue toward the end of whipping. If you are attempting a bold color, you will end up using quite a bit of dye. Start to incorporate your dye when the egg whites have soft peaks—this will help you avoid over-whisking the meringue if you need to add more color. If you find that you have used quite a bit of water-based dye, increase your drying time and baking time to compensate. Be aware that the color will fade slightly through whisking, mixing, resting, and baking. One trick I have learned is to use neon color dyes! You get bright results using much less dye.

Mindy Cone

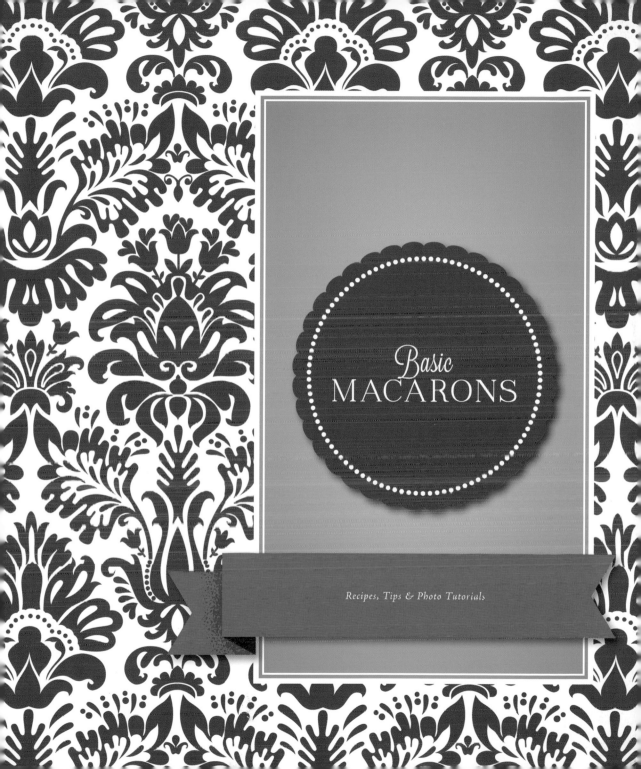

Basic
MACARONS

Recipes, Tips & Photo Tutorials

NOW YOU ARE READY TO MAKE YOUR FIRST BATCH OF
• *Basic Macarons* •

THE RECIPE BELOW is for basic almond-flavored macarons that can be colored to match any flavor profile filling! While the ingredients change a bit with the variation recipes, the technique and tips are still applicable. For the macarons in the photos, I added a bit of brown food dye to add definition and to make features at certain steps more visible; however, the shells produced with this recipe will be off-white.

200g powdered sugar
110g almond flour
100g egg whites aged
        at room temperature

pinch cream of tartar
35g superfine sugar

1. MEASURE out all ingredients and set aside.

Tip

Measure all ingredients with a digital scale to ensure consistency.

2. PREPARE the baking sheets by lining them with a silicone mat, parchment paper, or both (see tool description on page 7 to help decide what is best for you). Slide your printed template sheet underneath the parchment paper and set aside. Prepare piping bag to be filled and set aside.

Mindy Cone

Tip

If your parchment paper is rolling, use small magnets in the corners to keep the edges flat. Remove right before placing in the oven.

3. SIFT powdered sugar and almond flour 2 or 3 times through a sieve and set aside. Discard large almond pieces that remain in sieve.

 *This mixture is called* tant pour tant—*meaning half almond flour and half powdered sugar.*

4. PLACE the egg whites in a large bowl or in a stand mixer with wire whisk attachment. Whisk on low speed until egg whites become foamy. Add the pinch of cream of tartar. Continue to whisk on medium-low until soft peaks form. Slowly add in the superfine sugar. Once all of the sugar is incorporated, scrape down the sides with a spatula.

 *The whipped egg whites are called* meringue.

5. TURN your mixer on medium-high and continue to whip until peaks begin to form. Slow down your speed and check your egg whites periodically until you reach a stiff meringue. If adding liquid or gel food dye, do so toward the end of whisking.

Tip

Knowing when to stop whisking is one of the most important decisions when making a macaron. It is *not* possible to rescue a macaron that has been under-whisked. It *is* possible to salvage a macaron batter that has been over-whisked. When in doubt, whisk it a little more.

15

Gourmet French Macarons

Tip

To check your meringue, remove your whisk attachment, give the whisk a good swipe around the entire bowl, and lift up to observe the peak. The peak created in the meringue should fold over itself just at the tip. The meringue will begin to lose its gloss and have a dull sheen when it is ready. If the meringue falls too quickly or has a highly glossy appearance, whisk for another minute and check again.

Tip

Coloring your batter: Be sure to review the food coloring section on page 12 to determine what type of dye to use and when to incorporate it.

6. SIFT ⅓ of the almond flour and powdered sugar mixture through the sieve into the meringue. Fold the dry mixture into the meringue. Repeat with the remaining mixture. Once all of the dry ingredients are incorporated, the batter will be thick and have a dull appearance. Continue to fold, pressing out air bubbles along the bottom or sides of the bowl after each turn. As you do so, the batter will loosen. Stop folding when the batter has a glossy sheen, has a lava-like consistency, and falls in ribbons off the spatula.

Terminology

The process of folding the tant pour tant *into the meringue is called* macaronnage.

Mindy Cone

Tip

W hen to stop folding—this is the other *very* important decision in making a great macaron. Too many folds and your batter will be runny and produce cracked or hollow macarons. However, too few folds will produce a thick batter with peaks or high domes, it will cook unevenly, and it will crack.

Your batter will be ready when it falls off your spatula in a thick lava-like stream. It will collect on top of itself in the bowl, making ribbon lines that should disappear after 30 seconds. When you place the batter into the piping bag, it should only slightly ooze out of the tip.

Many recipes will give you a specific number of folds for the perfect batter. I hesitate to do this because, quite simply, everyone folds differently. It is more important to recognize when the batter has the correct consistency than to count the number of folds.

7. TRANSFER the batter into a large pastry bag fitted with a round tip and pipe 1½-inch rounds on the parchment paper, following the templates underneath.

Tip

Be sure to read the section on piping techniques and how to use the templates (page 23).

8. WHEN all of the rounds are piped on the parchment, rap the sheet pans evenly on the work surface a few times to release any trapped air and encourage the batter to spread evenly. Remove templates from below your parchment paper carefully. Let the batter rest at room temperature for 20–40 minutes.

Gourmet French Macarons

The wait time for macarons may vary based on the temperature and humidity in your kitchen. Macarons will be ready to bake when a dull skin forms over the top and they no longer stick to your finger when lightly pressed.

8. PREHEAT oven to 350 degrees. Reduce temperature to 300 degrees and bake one sheet at a time for 10 minutes, rotating the pan halfway through.

Tip

Check your macarons before removing them from the oven. If you gently press down and the top wiggles, then cook for another minute and recheck. They will be ready when they are firm with little side-to-side movement.

Macarons should *not* brown. All ovens are different. I suggest getting an oven thermometer to be sure your oven is accurate. Baking times will also vary depending on humidity. When in doubt, overbake your macarons instead of underbaking them. A longer maturation process in the refrigerator with a filling can compensate for an overcooked macaron.

Rotating halfway through will help the macarons cook evenly and reduce browning along the foot of the macaron. These baking temperatures and times are based off a conventional oven. Convection ovens will use a lower temperature and shorter baking time.

Mindy Cone

9. REMOVE sheet from oven and allow to cool for 5 minutes before removing from the parchment.

10. MATCH UP similar-sized shells into pairs and sandwich with filling (pages 205–247) of your choice.

For quick assembly, line up the pairs with one shell facing up and the other facing down. Pipe the filling onto the shells with the flat side up. Then place the matching shell on top and gently press them together so the filling just hits the edge of the shells.

Shells can be filled immediately after they are cooled, or they can be stored unfilled in an airtight container in the refrigerator for up to 4 days.

MAKES: One recipe makes about 4 dozen 1–1½-inch shells, which means 2 dozen sandwiched macaron cookies.

TIME:

10 minutes—Prep ingredients and materials
30 minutes—Make and pipe macaron shells
30 minutes—Rest time
10 minutes—Baking time

5 minutes—Cool
5 minutes—Fill and sandwich
(with a prepared filling)

STORAGE: Filled macarons can be stored in an airtight container for up to a week. They are *best* after about 12 hours in the fridge and then warmed to room temperature . . . if you can wait that long! They can be frozen for up to a month in an airtight container.

19

Variation
MACARON SHELL RECIPES

W HILE THE BULK OF THE FLAVOR PROFILE of a macaron will be in the filling, the shell can provide an opportunity to complement or echo the filling beautifully and add a delicate complexity and depth of flavor. These shell variations follow the same technique as the basic macaron. Liquid extracts and flavorings should be added to the meringues toward the end of the whipping process (at the same time you add the coloring). Powdered flavorings and flour should be added to the *tant pour tant* in the food processor or as you sift the dry ingredients.

• VANILLA BEAN •

200g powdered sugar
110g almond flour
100g egg whites
   at room temperature
pinch cream of tartar

35g superfine sugar
$^3/_4$ tsp. vanilla bean extract
(or 1 tsp. vanilla extract or seeds
from a vanilla bean)

• CHOCOLATE •

200g powdered sugar
110g almond flour
10g cocoa powder

100g egg whites
   at room temperature
pinch cream of tartar
35g superfine sugar

* Add two minutes baking time for these.

20

Mindy Cone

• CINNAMON •

200g powdered sugar
110g of almond flour
1 $^1/_2$ tsp. cinnamon
100g egg whites
   at room temperature

pinch ream of tartar
35g superfine sugar

• PISTACHIO •

200g powdered sugar
70g almond flour
40g pistachio flour
(ground pistachio with the shell and skin removed)

100g egg whites
   at room temperature
pinch cream of tartar
35g superfine sugar

• HAZELNUT •

200g powdered sugar
70g almond flour
40g hazelnut flour
100g egg whites
   at room temperature

pinch cream of tartar
35g superfine sugar

Gourmet French Macarons

Piping
TECHNIQUES & TEMPLATES

PREP TO PIPE

I ALWAYS SET UP MY PIPING MATERIALS before I start to make macaron batter. That way it can go right into the bags without sitting on the counter. As stated before, I recommend a 16-inch piping bag fitted with a round tip (¾ cm) for a full recipe of macarons. To fill your pastry bag, fold or twist the tip so that no batter will escape and place the bag tip down into a large drinking glass. Fold the top fourth of the bag over the edge and fill with batter.

Your baking sheets should be prepared with the templates under the parchment paper and magnets along the edges to keep it flat. Twist the top of the pastry bag and pinch the twist between your thumb and index finger of your dominant hand. Allow the rest of your hand to grasp the bag and gently apply pressure to the filling. Use your nondominant hand to guide and steady the tip. After piping a few macarons, you will need to twist the bag down more to maintain pressure.

PIPING BASIC MACARONS WITH A CIRCLE TEMPLATE

Hold your filled pastry bag vertical over the center of the circle and about ½ inch above the parchment paper. Begin piping

23

by gently applying pressure to the bag, and the batter will flow out concentrically to the edge of the template. Once the batter has reached the inside of the template line, release pressure on the pastry bag and lift upward, finishing with a twist to release the batter from the tip. The batter will slowly spread, so if you want the size to be exactly the size of the template, you will need to release the batter slightly inside the lines. Repeat until you have piped the whole tray.

WHY USE A TEMPLATE?

When I started making macarons, I didn't use a template. I was frustrated at the inconsistent size and doneness of them . . . not to mention that some of them were too close and would run into each other. Apparently I don't have a good eye for measurement! All the recipes out there suggested drawing out circles on your parchment paper—that didn't seem efficient to me. So I decided to make a template on my computer and print it out. That way I could use the templates each time and ensure they would be the same size, bake evenly, and be the proper distance apart.

Once I established a routine of using templates, it dawned on me to mix up the shapes! I started making hearts, flowers, footballs, and other basic shapes using templates. Then I started to incorporate different colors—making rainbows, cupcakes, ice cream cones! A whole world of creativity opened up to me! It was so much fun to develop a template and test out my ideas in the kitchen. I was creating macarons that were colorful, exciting, different—and still tasted amazing!

It is particularly important to use a template when making uniquely shaped macarons to ensure that the extremities and details line up. It is also very important to note that some of the shapes in this book are symmetrical (if you cut them down the middle it would produce a mirror image on each side), and others are asymmetrical. For symmetrical shapes—butterfly, heart, football, balloon, egg—the template shape is the same throughout the page. However, for asymmetrical shapes—duck, ghost, candy cane—the template will have half the images

Mindy Cone

facing one way and half the other. This way, when they are baked and removed from the parchment to sandwich, they will line up. The templates are prepared depending on the symmetry of each shape. No need to think too hard about it—I've got you covered!

HOW TO USE THE TEMPLATES

The template files are all on the CD that accompanies this book. Just place the CD in your computer and pull up the main screen with all the files. The files are labeled based on what shape or design you are making. The page in the book that describes how to make that macaron will list the template file name to look for. Templates should be printed on a regular 8½ × 11 sheet of paper. A standard cookie sheet will fit two printed templates. Once you have printed the number of templates you will need, place the template under your parchment paper, secure with magnets, and you are ready to pipe! Follow the tips and instructions given for each specific template. Remember to remove your templates when you are finished piping and before you rest your macarons. If you wait until after the rest period, you could break the skin that has formed when removing the templates, which will lead to cracking when they cook.

PIPING UNIQUELY SHAPED MACARONS WITH TEMPLATES

Each uniquely shaped macaron will have a specific template and set of directions. However, some general rules and tips should be followed when piping noncircular shapes.

- IN GENERAL, pipe the largest sections of the shape first. Working on 3–4 macaron shells at a time is ideal. This gives enough time for the batter to spread slightly but not long enough for a skin to form.

- IN GENERAL, work from the main body of the shape outward. This will accommodate for how the batter spreads and give you a more defined and even outline of the shape.

- USE DIFFERENT TIPS: By using a coupler on your pastry bag, you can easily change the tip size if you need to do any detail work.

25

Gourmet French Macarons

- WHEN MAKING SHAPES that have corners or points, be aware that you will not be able to get a sharp edge due to the nature of the batter. To pipe a corner, ease up on the piping bag when at the corner and begin applying pressure as you pipe away from the corner again. Be careful not to drag the tip, use too little batter, or tilt your pastry bag in the corner—this will cause the tip to cling to the parchment paper and rise unevenly.

- HAVE CLEAN TOOTHPICKS HANDY! When working on fine points such as cat ears or duck beaks, a toothpick can be very handy. By piping a small dollop of batter onto the parchment, you can manipulate the batter to create a small triangle. Be sure not to drag the toothpick along the parchment paper. Pull the toothpick upward and outward with the batter to create a point.

Mindy Cone

Working
WITH MULTIPLE COLORS

A S YOU MASTER THE ART OF MAKING MACARONS—and particularly unique macarons—you will run into some color dilemmas. How do you make more than one color? Can you use one batch for multiple colors? What if I only need a small amount of one color? This section will answer these questions and help you form a plan before you begin.

MAKING MORE THAN ONE COLOR

The best recommendation for making more than one color is to split the colors from the start. Measure out everything for each color and make them separately. If you don't want a full batch of each color, then make a half batch—I do this all the time! Keeping them separate is the most accurate way to ensure your macaron batter will have the right consistency. This works great if you need even amounts of 2–3 colors . . . but it will make for a few more dishes!

The next best option is to split the batter during folding. Right after you have incorporated all of the dry ingredients and the batter is very thick, you can split it into as many separate bowls as needed. Add the color and fold each bowl to the proper consistency. The upside here is that you can choose the volume of each color that you need! If you need a small amount of one color or want an ombré effect, this is the best method. The downside here is that you only have one shot at the color or you risk overmixing the batter! Only do this if you are comfortable with the food dye or have flexibility with the shade of color. The most important thing is to have a plan and think about your colors beforehand. How many will you need? How much of each color will you need? Can I build from one color to the next? For example, can I make a yellow batter and then divide part of that off to make red and part to make green with the addition of more dye? Can I use a combination of the two methods described? Using more than one color definitely requires more planning, but the result is worth it!

27

COMBINING COLORS

Combining two different macaron batters into the same shell can produce an amazing design. It can be as simple as using two shades of green and piping a four-leaf clover or as intricate as using seven colors for a rainbow on a cloud! Prepare all of the colored batter and separate into different piping bags before you begin. Be sure to use couplers in case you need to switch out the tip through the process. Since you will be switching colors often, tie the back of each piping bag with a small rubber band so you will not have the batter spread out the back every time you set it down. Each unique shape will have specific directions to follow for piping the different colors. The color will not bleed from one batter to the next when they are piped, rested, or baked.

By layering multiple colors, you can achieve a two- or three-dimensional look. Nearly all of the designs in this book can be made into either of these looks—the difference will depend on when you apply the layers of batter. Two-dimensional designs include (among others) shamrock, rainbow, cow, ice cream cone, and watermelon macarons. In these examples, the colors are piped one after another in a short period of time. I usually work with 3 or 4 macarons at a time—piping one color and then going back over them with any remaining colors one at a time. As you do this, the batters will spread into each other seamlessly to create one macaron shell. You will find that the batters like to stick to each other—this makes piping small details difficult. I have found it easier to pipe a dollop of batter and then manipulate it with a toothpick into the desired shape.

Three-dimensional designs, like on the Thanksgiving pie slice macarons, are achieved by waiting longer to pipe the second layer of batter. Depending on the humidity in your kitchen, I recommend piping the entire pan with your first layer and then waiting five minutes to apply the next. This allows a slight skin to form on the first layer so that it will not merge with the new layer. Another way to achieve a three-dimensional appearance is by manipulating the stiffness of your batter. When you undermix your batter, the thickness can leave streaks or peaks as you pipe a shape. While this is usually undesirable for macaron batter, in this instance it is a good thing! When piping pumpkin macarons and cloud macarons, for example, the peaks and streaks make the design even better!

Mindy Cone

Decorative
TECHNIQUES & IDEAS

I AM SURE YOU HAVE SEEN MACARONS with a small dusting of cinnamon, some crushed pistachio, a swipe of color, or perhaps a drizzle of chocolate. Well, that is just the tip of the iceberg, my friends! There are many options for embellishing and decorating your macarons that can bring simple or unique shapes to life—this is where you can let your creativity loose! Here I have listed multiple decorative techniques and ideas that are incorporated in various macarons in this book.

ICING

Color your icing yellow, and it can be mustard on a hot dog macaron. Leave it white, and it can be a snowflake on a macaron in a winter wonderland scene. Royal icing is a blank canvas for your creativity! My royal icing recipe is below, but any recipe will work—just add water until you reach the desired consistency. Plastic bags are great substitutes for piping bags—especially when you are only using a little bit of icing for decoration or as glue for larger decorative items. Simply place the icing in the corner of the bag, twist behind it, and snip the corner. If you want more control over the detail, use a piping bag and a small round tip, which can be used to pipe letters, decorative swirls, zigzags, or polka dots. This was how I created the designs on the decorative Easter eggs, cupcakes, sports balls, and monogrammed macarons. Other than royal icing, I often use premade writing gel. This can be found at a grocery, craft, or baking store. I used this to create the designs on the ladybug and bee macarons.

• ROYAL ICING •

3 cups powdered sugar   water
2 Tbsp. meringue powder

Mix powdered sugar and meringue powder together. Add water one tablespoon at a time until you reach desired consistency.

29

Gourmet French Macarons

EDIBLE-INK PENS

These pens are one of my favorite tools for decorating macarons. They particularity come in handy when making adorable facial features. You can write directly onto a macaron shell, sprinkles, and even candy melts. You can see examples of using edible-ink pens on the watermelon macarons, conversation heart macarons, and more. They come in myriad colors, but at the very least I recommend having a black one.

CANDY MELTS

Candy coating wafers, also known as Candy Melts, can found in your general craft or baking store. They are easy to use and have many decorative applications. You can melt these in a microwave-safe bowl or heat in a double boiler. Once melted, you can dip, drizzle, pipe, or mold the candy covering however you like.

 Dip

When dipping, be sure your macaron is filled and chilled so that the filling is firm. Prepare your Candy Melts and then remove macarons from the refrigerator. Macarons are delicate, so grip gently as you dip them into the melted candy coating, or it will crack. You can leave the macarons as is or add decoration with sprinkles. By doing this, you can bring in color to coordinate with any holiday, theme, or special event. It is also a great way to add texture to a design like the hair on the Frankenstein's monster macaron.

 Drizzle

Drizzling melted candy coating or even chocolate can add a beautiful decorative touch to a simple macaron batch. To do this, melt the candy coating

30

directly in a plastic bag in the microwave—place wafers in the corner of the bag and do not seal. Microwave on low for 30 seconds, remove bag, and knead. Repeat this until the coating is fully melted and warm. Twist bag and cut the corner. Drizzle over sandwiched and filled macarons. This method is how I created the mummy macarons!

 Pipe

Several of the unique macarons use piped Candy Melt decorations. This is how I constructed the bat wings, reindeer antlers, lion mane, and most of the fruit stems. Melt the coating in a plastic bag—the same way you would if you were drizzling (see above). Draw or print a template on a piece of paper and layer wax paper on top. Trace the template with the melted candy coating. Once it has hardened and cooled, it can be removed and placed in the filling or on top of the macaron.

 Mold

Candy Melts can also be used to fill molds. Candy molds come in a wide variety of sizes, shapes, and themes to fit any celebration. They are inexpensive and easy to use! Melt the candy coating, fill the mold, allow to cool, and you are done! Pop the candy out of the mold and adhere it to the top of a macaron with a little icing. The seashell macarons were made this way—easy and beautiful!

SPRINKLES

You will never view sprinkles the same way—jimmies will be whiskers and antennae, confetti sprinkles will be eyes, and hearts will be lips and bows! Sprinkles come in such a wide variety of colors and shapes that they lend themselves beautifully to anything your creativity can imagine. Seasonal sprinkles are a great way to add pizzazz to your macarons if you don't have a specific shape you want to make. If you don't have the sprinkle that a recipe calls for, you can often make do with what you have or even use icing for a similar effect.

Here are a few basics to have in your cupboard:

- Jimmies (brown or black and multicolored)
- Confetti sprinkles (be sure the mix includes white)
- Nonpareils
- Sugar pearls (white and black)
- Large sugar crystals
- Sanding sugar
- Hearts (multicolored)

Baking with Sprinkles:

Depending on the macaron shape and design, you may want to put sprinkles on before you bake. When doing so, place sprinkles on wet macarons right after you rap the sheet on the counter. If you try to place them after they have rested, the weight of the sprinkles may break the skin that has formed. This will lead to cracks during baking. Not all sprinkles hold up in the oven—sugar pearls will often melt, so put these on afterward.

CANDY EYES

If you are making a design that requires eyes—animals, monsters, babies—then buying candy eyes is a nice shortcut. You can also make your own by drawing black dots on white confetti sprinkles or placing a black sugar pearl on white icing.

32

Mindy Cone

CANDY, CHOCOLATE CHIPS, AND OTHER FOOD ITEMS

This list could go on forever! Candy, chocolate chips, pretzels, cookies—all of these can be manipulated into adorable decorations for macarons. Each design in this book will have directions for how to mold, cut, or shape these everyday items into something creative and unique.

Here is a list of some of the items used:

- Candy corn
- Colorful licorice
- Twizzlers Pull-n-Peel (red and green)
- Black rope licorice
- AirHeads
- M&M's
- Mini M&M's
- Skittles

- Starburst
- Candy necklace
- Necco Wafers
- Chocolate chips (regular and mini)
- Coconut
- Pretzel sticks
- Mini marshmallows
- Mini chocolate sandwich cookies
- Fruit Roll-Ups or Fruit by the foot

MACARON POPS

Everyone loves a treat on a stick—and macarons are no exception! This makes a great way to present and enjoy them. You can use lollipop sticks or even cute straws! I use them to display the balloon-shaped macarons and the baby rattle macarons, but you could use them for any of the shapes!

FONDANT

Use this material to make beautiful three-dimensional decorations such as the flowers on the wedding cake macaron, or roll out fondant and cut out shapes with small cookie cutters for a more simple design. Secure the fondant on top of filled macarons with a little bit of icing. You immediately have a polished, decorative look that can fit any color or theme! Fondant is also a great material to use in place of some of the candy decorations for details on various designs.

33

PAINTED MACARONS

Did you know you can use food dye gel to paint your macarons? It is a great way to introduce another color to your design without having to make additional batter! I used this technique when making the cherry pie macaron for the Thanksgiving spread. Dip a dry paintbrush into your food dye gel and paint directly onto the shell. You could also use this technique with edible glitter or shimmer dust. Dip a damp brush into the powder and paint directly onto the macaron shell. I used this method to give the wedding ring macarons their metallic luster.

TOOLS

How do you think I got all those whiskers in the right place? Or Starburst rolled out into feathers? I use many different tools through the decorative process! They help to move delicate decorations into place, smooth out or texturize Candy Melt surfaces, manipulate candy, or place small droplets of icing to adhere other decorations.

Of course, you can improvise with what you have, but here are some of my go-to tools.

- Toothpicks
- Scissors
- Tweezers
- Rolling pin
- Ruler
- Wax paper
- Paintbrushes

34

Mindy Cone

CLASSIC IDEAS

I would be remiss without mentioning some classic, simple, and beautiful decorating ideas. The most common is a delicate dusting on top of the shell to represent the flavor. For example, dust with crushed pistachio, cinnamon, toasted coconut, cocoa nibs, dry rose petals, lemon peel, sesame seeds, and more. This can be done before or after baking. If you are applying these after baking and are having trouble getting it to stick, run a damp food paintbrush over the top with water and apply again. Another common decoration is a brushstroke of chocolate or coloring to represent the flavor profile. Both ideas are extremely elegant and classic.

Now that you know how to make traditional macarons, let's have some fun! The following pages contain over 75 macarons —with festive and unique designs to fit any season, holiday, or celebration!

Seasonal & Holiday
MACARONS

With these fun seasonal designs, every holiday spread can include macarons!

HEARTS

Love is in the air with these heart-shaped macarons! A wonderful treat or gift for Valentine's Day for that special someone in your life! While this design is simple, you can always boost the creativity by using shades of pink and red in more intricate layered designs.

Additional Materials Needed

pink food dye

toothpicks

Filling Recommendation:

Shown here with vanilla bean buttercream (page 206)..

LEVEL OF DIFFICULTY: Easy

Directions

1. PRINT TEMPLATE—Heart.

2. MIX SHELL BATTER—1 recipe basic macarons (page 14) colored pink.

3. PIPE—Start with your tip on one of the top sides of the heart shape. Squeeze bag as if you are piping a round. Slightly release pressure and move the tip down toward the end of the heart. Release batter at the point of the heart and repeat this process on the other side. Use a toothpick to pull the batter down into the point and upward off the parchment at the very tip.

4. REST—at room temperature for about 30 minutes, depending on humidity of kitchen.

5. BAKE—Preheat oven to 325 degrees. Place one cookie sheet in oven and reduce oven temperature to 275 degrees. Set timer for 7 minutes. Rotate pan. Cook another 7 minutes or until macarons are cooked through. Allow to cool and then remove.

Gourmet French Macarons

HUG ME

Cutie Pie

CALL ME

XOXO

LOVE YOU

Q

Makes 15-20

conversation heart

sandwiched macarons

CONVERSATION HEARTS

XOXO! Be Mine! Use edible-ink pens to dress up simple heart-shaped macarons into conversation hearts for Valentine's Day!

Additional Materials Needed

blue, orange, yellow, green, purple, and pink food dye

toothpicks

red edible-ink pen

Filling Recommendation:

Shown here with vanilla bean buttercream (page 206).

LEVEL OF DIFFICULTY:
Easy

Directions

1. PRINT TEMPLATE—Heart.

2. MIX SHELL BATTER—1 recipe basic macarons (page 14) divided and colored light blue, orange, yellow, green, purple, pink, and white.

3. PIPE—Start with your tip on one of the top sides of the heart shape. Squeeze bag as if you are piping a round. Slightly release pressure and move the tip down toward the end of the heart. Release batter at the point of the heart and repeat this process on the other side. Use a toothpick to pull the batter down into the point and upward off the parchment at the very tip.

4. REST—at room temperature for about 30 minutes, depending on humidity of kitchen.

5. BAKE—Preheat oven to 325 degrees. Place one cookie sheet in oven and reduce oven temperature to 275 degrees. Set timer for 7 minutes. Rotate pan. Cook another 7 minutes or until macarons are cooked through. Allow to cool and then remove.

6. DECORATE—Once the shells have cooled, use edible-ink pens to write conversation heart phrases directly on the shells.

Gourmet French Macarons

SHAMROCKS

You'll have the luck of the Irish on St. Patrick's Day with these four-leaf clovers!

Additional Materials Needed

green food dye

green Candy Melts

pretzel sticks

wax paper

Filling Recommendation:

Shown here with
pistachio buttercream
(page 207).

LEVEL OF DIFFICULTY:
Intermediate

Directions

1. PRINT TEMPLATE—Shamrock.

2. MIX SHELL BATTER—1 recipe pistachio macarons (page 21) divided and colored two shades of green.

3. PIPE—Pipe half of each clover petal at a time. Start with your tip on one side of the end of the petal where it is most broad. Gently squeeze your piping bag and pull the tip inward to the center releasing pressure as you go and reducing the batter flow toward the center. Release batter from tip in the center of the shape. Repeat this process for the other side of the petal. Then repeat this for the reaming three petals of the clover. Do not pipe a stem.

4. REST—at room temperature for about 30 minutes, depending on humidity of kitchen.

5. BAKE—Preheat oven to 350 degrees. Place one cookie sheet in oven and reduce temperature to 300 degrees. Set timer for 5 minutes. Rotate pan. Cook another 5 minutes or until macarons are cooked through. Allow to cool and then remove.

6. DECORATE—To make the stems for the clover, melt 4 ounces of green Candy Melts. Lay out pretzel sticks on wax paper and cover them with melted candy. Allow to cool and then remove from wax paper.

Gourmet French Macarons

SHAMROCK CIRCLES

Additional
Materials Needed

green food dye

toothpicks

Filling Recommendation:
Shown here with
pistachio buttercream
(page 207).

Directions

1. PRINT TEMPLATE—1½-inch circle.

2. MIX SHELL BATTER—1 recipe pistachio macarons (page 21) divided and colored two shades of green.

3. PIPE—Pipe 1½-inch circle. Using the other shade of green, pipe 4 small drops of batter in clover shape. Using a toothpick, drag some of the clover batter outward to create the stem shape. For each clover shell created, pipe a plain shell for the back in either color.

4. REST—at room temperature for about 30 minutes, depending on humidity of kitchen.

5. BAKE—Preheat oven to 350 degrees. Place one cookie sheet in oven and reduce temperature to 300 degrees. Set timer for 5 minutes. Rotate pan. Cook another 5 minutes or until macarons are cooked through. Allow to cool and then remove.

Gourmet French Macarons

Makes
9

rainbow   sandwiched
              macarons

RAINBOWS

Cheerful and bright, this design is perfect for St. Patrick's Day or even a rainbow birthday party!

Additional
Materials Needed

red, orange, yellow, green, blue, and purple food dye

Filling Recommendation:

Shown here with marshmallow filling (page 238).

LEVEL OF DIFFICULTY:
Advanced

Directions

1. PRINT TEMPLATE—Rainbow.

2. MIX SHELL BATTER—1 recipe basic macarons (page 14) divided and colored red, orange, yellow, green, blue, and purple. ½ recipe basic macarons (page 14) without coloring.

3. PIPE—I recommend working with one or two macarons at a time. Start by piping the red rainbow ring first, followed by orange, yellow, green, and blue. You do not need to follow the size of the lines exactly. Finally, pipe a small purple half circle to fill in the center space. Use the white batter to create a cloud across the bottom. The template shows the cloud on the ends of the rainbow, but I have found it best to pipe the cloud all the way across. To pipe the cloud, hold your bag vertical and pipe small rounds that overlap the rainbow and each other. As the batter spreads, it will give the appearance of a fluffy, rounded cloud outline.

4. REST—at room temperature for about 30 minutes, depending on humidity of kitchen.

5. BAKE—Preheat oven to 325 degrees. Place one cookie sheet in oven and reduce temperature to 275 degrees. Set timer for 7 minutes. Rotate pan. Cook another 7 minutes or until macarons are cooked through. Allow to cool and then remove.

Gourmet French Macarons

easter egg — Makes **14–18** — sandwiched macarons

DECORATIVE EASTER EGGS

Use royal icing to give these simple Easter egg shapes some extra decorative flair!

Additional
Materials Needed

yellow, orange, green, purple,
and pink food dye

white royal icing (page 29)

Filling Recommendation:

Shown here with
vanilla buttercream (page 206).

LEVEL OF DIFFICULTY:
Easy

Directions

1. PRINT TEMPLATE—Easter Egg.

2. MIX SHELL BATTER—1 recipe basic macarons (page 14) divided and colored yellow, orange, green, purple, and pink.

3. PIPE—Begin at the top of the egg piping as if piping a circle. Continue and move the tip down the center of the template. Increase pressure on the piping bag to increase flow of batter as you move downward toward the larger end of the egg.

4. REST—at room temperature for about 30 minutes, depending on humidity of kitchen.

5. BAKE—Preheat oven to 325 degrees. Place one cookie sheet in oven and reduce temperature to 300 degrees. Set timer for 6 minutes. Rotate pan. Cook another 5 minutes or until macarons are cooked through. Allow to cool and then remove.

6. DECORATE—Use royal icing to add decorative stripes, polka dots, and zigzags to your Easter eggs.

49

Gourmet French Macarons

SWIMMING DUCKS

Adorable for springtime, Easter, or even a baby shower!
These swimming girl and boy ducks are perfect!

Directions

1. PRINT TEMPLATE—Duck.

2. MIX SHELL BATTER—1 recipe basic macarons (page 14)
colored yellow and a small amount colored orange.

3. PIPE—You will notice that the template has ducks facing either
way since this shape is not symmetrical. The page has an even
number of each—just be sure if you don't have enough batter to do
the whole page that you pipe the same amount facing each way.

Using the yellow batter, pipe the body of the duck first. I recommend
piping 3 or 4 at a time. Start with the head of the duck by piping a
regular circle macaron. Pick up the tip and start again with the body of
the duck moving from left to right and finishing with the tail. Use the
orange batter to go back and pipe the beak. I recommend piping a small
dollop and using a toothpick to maneuver the batter into a triangular
beak shape.

4. REST—at room temperature for about 30 minutes, depending
on humidity of kitchen.

5. BAKE—Preheat oven to 325 degrees. Place one cookie sheet
in oven and reduce temperature to 300 degrees. Set timer for 6
minutes. Rotate pan. Cook another 5 minutes or until macarons are
cooked through. Allow to cool and then remove.

6. DECORATE—Use a small amount of royal icing to secure a
black sugar pearl as the eye. For girl ducks, use the black edible-ink
pen to draw eyelashes around the eye.

Gourmet French Macarons

Easter
bunny

Makes
10–12

sandwiched
macarons

EASTER BUNNIES

These bunnies may be too cute to eat! Use brown
jimmy sprinkles to create three-dimensional whiskers!

Additional
Materials Needed

pink food dye

royal icing (page 29)

black sugar pearls

brown or black jimmy
sprinkles

white and pink heart
sprinkles

Filling Recommendation:

Shown here with marshmal-
low filling (page 238), but
they also look great with
a chocolate ganache (page
212), chocolate buttercream
(page 206), or, my favorite,
chocolate Swiss meringue
(page 211).

Directions

1. PRINT TEMPLATE—Easter Bunny.

2. MIX SHELL BATTER—1 recipe basic macarons (page 14).
Divide and color half pink.

3. PIPE—Use either color batter and begin with the bunny ears.
Start at the top and move down the ear, ending as you reach the face
of the bunny. Repeat for the second ear. To pipe the face, start in the
center as if piping a circle macaron.

4. REST—at room temperature for about 30 minutes, depending
on humidity of kitchen.

5. BAKE—Preheat oven to 325 degrees. Place one cookie sheet
in oven and reduce temperature to 275 degrees. Set timer for 6
minutes. Rotate pan. Cook another 6 minutes or until macarons are
cooked through. Allow to cool and then remove.

6. DECORATE—Use royal icing to add detail on the ears and to
attach the black sugar pearl eyes. Pipe royal icing on the cheeks and,
while they are still wet, add the heart-shaped sprinkle for a nose and
jimmy sprinkles as whiskers.

LEVEL OF DIFFICULTY:
Intermediate

Gourmet French Macarons

CARROTS

What goes better with the Easter bunny (page 53) than a bunch of delicious carrot cake macarons?

Additional
Materials Needed

orange and green
food dye

toothpicks

Filling Recommendation:

Shown here with
carrot cake filling (page 236).

LEVEL OF DIFFICULTY:
Easy

Directions

1. PRINT TEMPLATE—Carrot.

2. MIX SHELL BATTER—1 recipe basic (14), vanilla (20), or cinnamon macarons (21), colored orange and green.*

3. PIPE—Begin by piping the carrot with the orange batter first. Start in the center of the top and reduce the flow of batter as you move down the middle of the carrot toward the end. Using the green batter, pipe three lines for the stems. Start at the end and pipe toward the orange batter. If needed, use a toothpick to maneuver the batter. Keep the area where the carrot and the stems join at least ½ inch. I have found that if this area is too skinny, they will crack when baking.

4. REST—at room temperature for about 30 minutes, depending on humidity of kitchen.

5. BAKE—Preheat oven to 350 degrees. Place one cookie sheet in oven and reduce temperature to 300 degrees. Set timer for 5 minutes. Rotate pan. Cook another 5 minutes or until macarons are cooked through. Allow to cool and then remove.

* For added texture to the design, undermix your batter so it leaves lines on the carrot!

Gourmet French Macarons

BABY CHICKS

These sweet baby chick macarons are the perfect spring treat!

Additional
Materials Needed

yellow food dye

royal icing (page 29)

black sugar pearls

orange AirHeads or Starburst

yellow licorice

spoon

orange heart sprinkles

Filling Recommendation:

Shown here with marshmallow filling (page 238).

LEVEL OF DIFFICULTY:
Intermediate

Directions

1. PRINT TEMPLATE—Baby Chicks.

2. MIX SHELL BATTER—1 recipe basic macarons (page 14) colored yellow.

3. PIPE—While this is a simple shape, it is a surprisingly difficult macaron to pipe evenly. I have found that what has the most success is starting from the top with a little pressure and then moving downward increasing pressure, and then decreasing pressure toward the end. It may take practice with one or two to get an even oval shape.

4. REST—at room temperature for about 30 minutes, depending on humidity of kitchen.

5. BAKE—Preheat oven to 325 degrees. Place one cookie sheet in oven and reduce temperature to 300 degrees. Set timer for 7 minutes. Rotate pan. Cook another 6 minutes or until macarons are cooked through. Allow to cool and then remove.

6. DECORATE—Use royal icing to adhere black sugar pearls as eyes. Cut AirHeads or Starburst into triangles for beaks and adhere with a little royal icing. Cut yellow licorice down the center and press flat. Use a spoon, or any other curved shape, to cut out the wings in a half circle. Use royal icing to adhere licorice as wings and two orange heart sprinkles as feet.

57

Gourmet French Macarons

SUNSHINE

yellow food dye

edible-ink pens—black and red

paintbrush

edible glitter dust

yellow Candy Melts

wax paper

Filling Recommendation:

Shown here with lemon buttercream (page 208) and a lemon curd center (page 217).

LEVEL OF DIFFICULTY:
Intermediate

Directions

1. PRINT TEMPLATE—Circle: 1½-inch.

2. MIX SHELL BATTER—1 recipe basic macarons (page 14) colored yellow.

3. PIPE—Basic circular macarons.

4. REST—at room temperature for about 30 minutes, depending on humidity of kitchen.

5. BAKE—Preheat oven to 350 degrees. Place one cookie sheet in oven and reduce temperature to 300 degrees. Set timer for 5 minutes. Rotate pan. Cook another 5 minutes or until macarons are cooked through. Allow to cool and then remove.

6. DECORATE—Use the edible-ink pens to draw a smiley face directly on the shell. Dip a damp paintbrush into the edible glitter dust and paint glittery cheeks on the shell. To make the rays of the sun, heat yellow candy melts in an unzipped plastic bag. Heat in microwave for 30 seconds on low. Take the bag out and knead. Repeat until warm and melted. Draw an outline of the ray shape on a piece of paper. Be sure that the inside circle is smaller than the macaron shells so that it can be sandwiched in the middle by them. Place wax paper over drawing, snip the corner of the plastic bag, and pipe melted candy over the drawing. Allow to cool and remove from wax paper. Place in between shells. The filling will help keep the rays in place.

Gourmet French Macarons

RAIN CLOUDS

Additional
Materials Needed

blue food dye

toothpicks

Filling Recommendation:
Shown here with
marshmallow filling (page 238).

LEVEL OF DIFFICULTY:
Easy

Directions

1. PRINT TEMPLATE—Cloud and Raindrops.

2. MIX SHELL BATTER—½ recipe basic macarons (page 14) colored blue, and ½ recipe basic macarons (page 14) uncolored and slightly undermixed to give the clouds more texture.

3. PIPE—To pipe the clouds, hold your bag vertical and pipe small rounds that overlap each other, following the outline of the template. As the batter spreads, it will give the appearance of a fluffy, rounded cloud outline.

To pipe the raindrops, start at the bottom where the drop is widest. Pipe as if you were making a circle, but move your tip upward as you decrease pressure on your piping bag. Use a toothpick to pull the batter up into the point and upward off the parchment at the very tip.

4. REST—at room temperature for about 30 minutes, depending on humidity of kitchen.

5. BAKE—Preheat oven to 350 degrees. Place one cookie sheet in oven and reduce temperature to 300 degrees. Set timer for 4 minutes. Rotate pan. Cook another 3 minutes or until macarons are cooked through. Allow to cool and then remove.

Gourmet French Macarons

Makes
6–9

tree   sandwiched
                                        macarons

TREES

Additional Materials Needed

green and brown food dye

Filling Recommendation:

Shown here with marshmallow filling (page 238).

LEVEL OF DIFFICULTY: *Easy*

Directions

1. PRINT TEMPLATE—Tree.

2. MIX SHELL BATTER—1 recipe basic macarons (page 14) divided and colored ¾ green and ¼ brown.

3. PIPE—To pipe the top of the tree, hold your bag of green batter vertical and pipe small rounds that overlap each other, following the outline of the template. Repeat this to fill in the middle. As the batter spreads, it will give the appearance of a rounded treetop. To pipe the trunk of the tree with brown batter, start at the base of the treetop and move downward.

4. REST—at room temperature for about 30 minutes, depending on humidity of kitchen.

5. BAKE—Preheat oven to 325 degrees. Place one cookie sheet in oven and reduce temperature to 275 degrees. Set timer for 7 minutes. Rotate pan. Cook another 7 minutes or until macarons are cooked through. Allow to cool and then remove.

63

spring flower

Makes
20–24

sandwiched macarons

SPRING FLOWERS

This is a fun and whimsical way to display spring flower macarons!
Of course, they look just as charming without the stems and flowerpots just placed on a platter.
I was inspired by the colors of daisies, but the concept can work with any color palate.

Additional
Materials Needed

For the flower macarons:

yellow food dye

Necco Wafers

For the display:

small flowerpots

Styrofoam ball
(sized to fit inside
the flower pot)

glue

green ribbon

lollipop stick

decorative green
shredded paper

LEVEL OF DIFFICULTY:
Easy*

*While the macarons are easy,
the display is intermediate.

Directions

1. PRINT TEMPLATE—Circle: 1½-inch.

2. MIX SHELL BATTER—1 recipe basic macarons (page 14) colored yellow.

3. PIPE—Basic circular macarons.

4. REST—at room temperature for about 30 minutes, depending on humidity of kitchen.

5. BAKE—Preheat oven to 350 degrees. Place one cookie sheet in oven and reduce temperature to 300 degrees. Set timer for 5 minutes. Rotate pan. Cook another 5 minutes or until macarons are cooked through. Allow to cool and then remove.

6. DECORATE—Pair up similar-sized macaron shells. Place one shell with the flat side up. Use a dollop of filling and secure wafers around the edge of the macaron as the flower petals. Top with more filling and then the paired shell.

To make the flowerpot display, start by gluing the Styrofoam ball to the inside of the pot. While that is drying, wrap the green ribbon around the lollipop stick and secure with glue. Tie a small bow near the center of the lollipop stick. Once dry, place the stick into a flower macaron and chill in the refrigerator. When ready to display, take the macaron out and place the stick in the Styrofoam ball. Decorate with green shredded paper to cover the Styrofoam.

Filling Recommendation:
Shown here with vanilla bean buttercream (page 206).

Gourmet French Macarons

LADYBUGS

My kids love insects and were over the moon about these cute ladybugs!

Additional Materials Needed

red food dye

black writing gel or
royal icing (page 29)

black jimmy sprinkles

white confetti sprinkles

Filling Recommendation:

Shown here with
dark chocolate ganache
(page 212).

LEVEL OF DIFFICULTY:
Easy

Directions

1. PRINT TEMPLATE—Circle: 1½-inch.

2. MIX SHELL BATTER—1 recipe basic macarons (page 14) colored red.

3. PIPE—Basic circle macarons.

4. REST—at room temperature for about 30 minutes, depending on humidity of kitchen.

5. BAKE—Preheat oven to 350 degrees. Place one cookie sheet in oven and reduce temperature to 300 degrees. Set timer for 5 minutes. Rotate pan. Cook another 5 minutes or until macarons are cooked through. Allow to cool and then remove.

6. DECORATE—Use the icing or gel to create the face of the ladybug, the line down the middle, and the spots. Also, place a small dot on the confetti sprinkle to create eyes. While the icing or gel is still wet, put in place the eyes and jimmy sprinkles as antennae.

Gourmet French Macarons

bee

Makes
20-24

sandwiched
macarons

BEES

Directions

1. PRINT TEMPLATE—Circle: 1½-inch.

2. MIX SHELL BATTER—1 recipe basic macarons (page 14) colored yellow.

3. PIPE—Basic circle macarons.

4. REST—at room temperature for about 30 minutes, depending on humidity of kitchen.

5. BAKE—Preheat oven to 350 degrees. Place one cookie sheet in oven and reduce temperature to 300 degrees. Set timer for 5 minutes. Rotate pan. Cook another 5 minutes or until macarons are cooked through. Allow to cool and then remove.

6. DECORATE—Use the icing or gel to create the stripes and the eyes. Also, place a small dot to secure the jimmy sprinkles as antennae. Slide the Necco Wafers into the filling as the wings. Use a small dollop of filling, icing, or gel to secure a chocolate chip on the back as a stinger.

Gourmet French Macarons

CATERPILLARS

Additional Materials Needed

red food dye

royal icing (page 29)

candy eyes

green Twizzlers
Pull-n-Peel candy

Filling Recommendation:

Shown here with
dark chocolate ganache
(page 212).

LEVEL OF DIFFICULTY:
Easy

Directions

1. PRINT TEMPLATE—Circle: 1½-inch.

2. MIX SHELL BATTER—1 recipe basic macarons (page 14) colored yellow.

3. PIPE—Basic circle macarons.

4. REST—at room temperature for about 30 minutes, depending on humidity of kitchen.

5. BAKE—Preheat oven to 350 degrees. Place one cookie sheet in oven and reduce temperature to 300 degrees. Set timer for 5 minutes. Rotate pan. Cook another 5 minutes or until macarons are cooked through. Allow to cool and then remove.

6. DECORATE—Use a small amount of royal icing to secure the candy eyes in place. Pull licorice apart and cut into 1½-inch pieces. Lay the licorice on the plate in pairs to represent the antennae and legs of the caterpillar. Place filled red macarons on top of the licorice.

HAMBURGERS

Summer is here, and it's time to barbecue!

Directions

1. PRINT TEMPLATE—Circle: 1½-inch.

2. MIX SHELL BATTER—1 recipe basic macarons (page 14) colored tan.

3. PIPE—Basic circle macarons.

4. REST—at room temperature for about 30 minutes, depending on humidity of kitchen.

5. BAKE—Preheat oven to 350 degrees. Place one cookie sheet in oven and reduce temperature to 300 degrees. Set timer for 5 minutes. Rotate pan. Cook another 5 minutes or until macarons are cooked through. Allow to cool and then remove.

6. DECORATE—Start by piping filling in a flat disk to resemble the patty. Place shredded coconut in a plastic bag with a few drops of green food dye. Seal and shake until coconut is colored green. Place a small amount on top of the filling. Use the red writing gel next to resemble a layer of ketchup. Top with the corresponding shell. Use a paintbrush dampened by water across the top of the shell. Sprinkle sesame seeds on top.

Gourmet French Macarons

Makes
16–20

hot dog   sandwiched
                           macarons

HOT DOGS

Additional
Materials Needed

brown and pink food dye

yellow royal icing (page 29)

Filling Recommendation:

Shown here with
marshmallow filling (page 238).

LEVEL OF DIFFICULTY:
Easy

Directions

1. PRINT TEMPLATE—Hot Dog Bun.

2. MIX SHELL BATTER—1 recipe basic macarons (page 14) colored tan.

3. PIPE—Start on one end of the template and move at an even speed with even pressure toward the other end.

4. REST—at room temperature for about 30 minutes, depending on humidity of kitchen.

5. BAKE—Preheat oven to 325 degrees. Place one cookie sheet in oven and reduce temperature to 300 degrees. Set timer for 6 minutes. Rotate pan. Cook another 5 minutes or until macarons are cooked through. Allow to cool and then remove.

6. DECORATE—Color the filling using brown and pink food dye. Mix until desired color is reached. The color will darken slightly as the macaron matures. Pipe filling in between shells so that you can see the filling from the side. Pipe a thin line of yellow royal icing down the middle to resemble mustard.

Gourmet French Macarons

WATERMELON SLICES

Additional
Materials Needed

red and green food dye

black edible-ink pen

Filling Recommendation:

Shown here with
watermelon buttercream
(page 219).

LEVEL OF DIFFICULTY:
Easy

Directions

1. PRINT TEMPLATE—Watermelon.

2. MIX SHELL BATTER—1 recipe basic macarons (page 14) colored ¾ red and ¼ green.

3. PIPE—Use the red batter first to pipe the inside of the watermelon. Use a smaller tip on your green piping bag and go along the outside of the red batter following the template.

4. REST—at room temperature for about 30 minutes, depending on humidity of kitchen.

5. BAKE—Preheat oven to 325 degrees. Place one cookie sheet in oven and reduce temperature to 300 degrees. Set timer for 5 minutes. Rotate pan. Cook another 5 minutes or until macarons are cooked through. Allow to cool and then remove.

6. DECORATE—Use a black edible-ink pen to draw seeds directly on the shell.

seashell
Makes
20-24
sandwiched
macarons

SEASHELLS & SANDY MACARONS

Nothing is better in the summer than a day at the beach! I was inspired to make these by how much brown sugar resembles sand—it's a perfect backdrop for these designs!

Additional Materials Needed

blue and green food dye

white Candy Melts

seashell candy molds

royal icing (page 29)

brown sugar

wax paper

Filling Recommendation:

Shown here with marshmallow filling (page 238). I think a snickerdoodle filling (page 233) or salted caramel filling (page 237) would be great too!

LEVEL OF DIFFICULTY:
Easy

Directions

1. PRINT TEMPLATE—Circle: 1½-inch.

2. MIX SHELL BATTER—1 recipe basic macarons (page 14) colored teal.

3. PIPE—Basic circular macarons.

4. REST—at room temperature for about 30 minutes, depending on humidity of kitchen.

5. BAKE—Preheat oven to 350 degrees. Place one cookie sheet in oven and reduce temperature to 300 degrees. Set timer for 5 minutes. Rotate pan. Cook another 5 minutes or until macarons are cooked through. Allow to cool and then remove.

6. DECORATE—For the seashell macarons, fill and place in refrigerator until filling is firm. Melt white candy coating and pour into molds. Remove seashells from the molds when cooled. Use a small amount of royal icing to secure the seashells to the top.

To make the "sand"-dipped macarons, begin by melting white candy coating. Dip a chilled macaron into it, then into brown sugar. Place on wax paper until candy coating has set.

fish or
wave

Makes
18–22

sandwiched
macarons

FISH & WAVES

blue and green food dye

toothpicks

white nonpareils

Filling Recommendation:

Shown here with
marshmallow filling (page 238).

I think a snickerdoodle filling
(page 233) or salted caramel
filling (page 237) would be
just great!

LEVEL OF DIFFICULTY:
Intermediate

Directions

1. PRINT TEMPLATE—Circle: 1½-inch.

2. MIX SHELL BATTER—½ recipe basic macarons (page 14) colored teal and ½ recipe basic macarons uncolored.

3. PIPE—For the fish macarons, pipe a basic circle with the white batter. Go back with the teal batter and pipe a fish outline in the middle of the white batter. Use a toothpick to maneuver the teal batter into place. Pipe a small eye with white batter. Sprinkle the white nonpareils to represent bubbles. For each fish shell created, pipe a plain shell for the back in either color.

To make the wave macaron, pipe half the circle white and the other half teal. Use a toothpick to pull the teal batter into wave shapes through the white batter. If needed, pipe small amounts of additional teal batter to create the wave. For each wave shell created, pipe a plain shell for the back in either color.

4. REST—at room temperature for about 30 minutes, depending on humidity of kitchen.

5. BAKE—Preheat oven to 350 degrees. Place one cookie sheet in oven and reduce temperature to 300 degrees. Set timer for 5 minutes. Rotate pan. Cook another 5 minutes or until macarons are cooked through. Allow to cool and then remove.

Gourmet French Macarons

BEACH BALLS

Additional Materials Needed

royal icing (page 29)

paintbrush

brightly colored
nonpareils (4 colors)

toothpicks

white confetti sprinkles

Filling Recommendation:

Shown here with
marshmallow filling (page 238).

LEVEL OF DIFFICULTY:
Intermediate

Directions

1. PRINT TEMPLATE—Circle: 1½-inch.

2. MIX SHELL BATTER—1 recipe basic macarons (page 14) uncolored.

3. PIPE—Basic circle macarons.

4. REST—at room temperature for about 30 minutes, depending on humidity of kitchen.

5. BAKE—Preheat oven to 350 degrees. Place one cookie sheet in oven and reduce temperature to 300 degrees. Set timer for 5 minutes. Rotate pan. Cook another 5 minutes or until macarons are cooked through. Allow to cool and then remove.

6. DECORATE—Paint royal icing into one triangle shape extending from the center of the macaron. Dip shell into or sprinkle with one color of nonpareils to fully cover the icing. Repeat this process for the three other colors. Use a toothpick to remove unwanted nonpareils and to keep the triangle lines straight. Use a dab of royal icing to secure a white confetti sprinkle to the center.

Gourmet French Macarons

FATHER'S DAY MUSTACHES

These make me laugh. Nothing is more manly than a mustache, right? Perfect for Father's Day!

Additional Materials Needed

toothpicks

Filling Recommendation:

Shown here with chocolate buttercream (page 206), but chocolate ganache (page 212) or chocolate Swiss meringue (page 211) would be great as well!

LEVEL OF DIFFICULTY: Easy

Directions

1. PRINT TEMPLATE—Mustache.

2. MIX SHELL BATTER—1 recipe chocolate macarons (page 14).

3. PIPE—Pipe half of the mustache at a time. Start in the middle and work your way outward following the template and reducing pressure toward the tip. Repeat on the other side. Use a toothpick to pull the batter into the tips and upward off the parchment.

4. REST—at room temperature for about 30 minutes, depending on humidity of kitchen.

5. BAKE—Preheat oven to 350 degrees. Place one cookie sheet in oven and reduce temperature to 300 degrees. Set timer for 6 minutes. Rotate pan. Cook another 5 minutes or until macarons are cooked through. Allow to cool and then remove.

Gourmet French Macarons

AMERICAN FLAGS

Celebrate independence with style!

Additional
Materials Needed

red and blue food dye

Filling Recommendation:

Shown here with
vanilla buttercream (page 206).

LEVEL OF DIFFICULTY:
Advanced

Directions

1. PRINT TEMPLATE—American Flag.

2. MIX SHELL BATTER—1 recipe basic macarons (page 14).
Leave half white and color ¼ red and the other ¼ blue.

3. PIPE—Start by piping the left corner blue. Then pipe the
remaining template with white batter. Use a small round tip for your
red batter to pipe stripes across the white batter. I recommend piping
only six stripes.

4. REST—at room temperature for about 30 minutes, depending
on humidity of kitchen.

5. BAKE—Preheat oven to 325 degrees. Place one cookie sheet in
oven and reduce temperature to 275 degrees. Set timer for 7 minutes.
Rotate pan. Cook another 6 minutes or until macarons are cooked
through. Allow to cool and then remove.

Gourmet French Macarons

PATRIOTIC STARS

Directions

1. PRINT TEMPLATE—Circle: 1½-inch.

2. MIX SHELL BATTER—1 recipe basic macarons (page 14). Leave ⅓ white, and color ⅓ red and ⅓ blue.

3. PIPE—Begin by piping a basic circle with the white batter. Pipe red or blue batter on top of the circle into the shape of a star. Use toothpicks to pull the batter into a point. For each star shell created, pipe a plain shell or corresponding color for the back.

4. REST—at room temperature for about 30 minutes, depending on humidity of kitchen.

5. BAKE—Preheat oven to 350 degrees. Place one cookie sheet in oven and reduce temperature to 300 degrees. Set timer for 5 minutes. Rotate pan. Cook another 5 minutes or until macarons are cooked through. Allow to cool and then remove.

Filling Recommendation:

Shown here with vanilla buttercream (page 206).

Level of Difficulty:
Intermediate

89

Gourmet French Macarons

Makes
20–24

fireworks
sandwiched
macarons

FIREWORKS

Additional
Materials Needed

royal icing (page 29)

red and blue sanding sugar

toothpicks

Filling Recommendation:

Shown here with
vanilla buttercream (page 206).

LEVEL OF DIFFICULTY:
Easy

Directions

1. PRINT TEMPLATE—Circle: 1½-inch.

2. MIX SHELL BATTER—1 recipe basic macarons (page 14) uncolored .

3. PIPE—Basic circle macarons.

4. REST—at room temperature for about 30 minutes, depending on humidity of kitchen.

5. BAKE—Preheat oven to 350 degrees. Place one cookie sheet in oven and reduce temperature to 300 degrees. Set timer for 5 minutes. Rotate pan. Cook another 5 minutes or until macarons are cooked through. Allow to cool and then remove.

6. DECORATE—Pipe royal icing into the shape of a firework. Dip shell into or sprinkle shell with red or blue sanding sugar.

Gourmet French Macarons

Makes
16–20

apple

sandwiched
macarons

"A" IS FOR APPLE

These apple macarons are perfect to celebrate going back to school or as teacher gifts!

Additional
Materials Needed

red food dye

green Candy Melts

leaf candy mold

pretzel sticks

Filling Recommendation:

Shown here with
apple cider filling (page 224).
Apple pie filling (page 222)
and salted caramel buttercream
(page 208) are other
great options!

LEVEL OF DIFFICULTY
Easy

Directions

1. PRINT TEMPLATE—Apple.

2. MIX SHELL BATTER—1 recipe basic macarons (page 14) or Cinnamon macaron (page 21) colored red.

3. PIPE—Although there are stems and leaves on the template, you will not be piping these. I recommend piping one half of the apple at a time. Start at the top and decrease the flow of batter as you go down. Repeat this on the other side.

4. REST—at room temperature for about 30 minutes, depending on humidity of kitchen.

5. BAKE—Preheat oven to 325 degrees. Place one cookie sheet in oven and reduce temperature to 300 degrees. Set timer for 6 minutes. Rotate pan. Cook another 5 minutes or until macarons are cooked through. Allow to cool and then remove.

6. DECORATE—Melt green candy coating and pour into leaf candy mold. Allow to cool and remove. Pipe filling onto open macaron shell and place a pretzel stick in for the stem. Pipe more filling on top and close with corresponding apple shell. Place the candy leaf next to the stem in the filling.

Gourmet French Macarons

LITTLE WHITE GHOSTS

These are so simple and fun to make! Use an edible-ink pen
to draw faces on the ghost macaron shells!

Additional
Materials Needed

black edible-ink pen

Filling Recommendation:

Shown here with
marshmallow filling (page 238).

LEVEL OF DIFFICULTY:
Easy

Directions

1. PRINT TEMPLATE—Ghost.

2. MIX SHELL BATTER—1 recipe basic macarons (page 14) uncolored.

3. PIPE—First, pipe the arms of the ghost. Then, starting at the top, pipe down the middle of the ghost and into the tail, easing off pressure toward the end.

4. REST—at room temperature for about 30 minutes, depending on humidity of kitchen.

5. BAKE—Preheat oven to 315 degrees. Place one cookie sheet in oven and reduce temperature to 275 degrees. Set timer for 8 minutes. Rotate pan. Cook another 7 minutes or until macarons are cooked through. Allow to cool and then remove.

6. DECORATE—Use the edible-ink pens to draw spooky and cute faces on the ghosts!

Gourmet French Macarons

CANDY CORN

A classic Halloween candy made into a macaron!

Additional
Materials Needed

orange and yellow food dye

toothpicks

Filling Recommendation:

Shown here with
candy corn buttercream
(page 227).

LEVEL OF DIFFICULTY:
Easy

Directions

1. PRINT TEMPLATE—Candy Corn.

2. MIX SHELL BATTER—1 recipe basic macarons (page 14) colored (divided) white, orange, and yellow.

3. PIPE —Start at the base with the yellow batter. Then pipe the orange, followed by the white. Use toothpicks to encourage the colors to join along the edges to obtain a straight line.

4. REST— at room temperature for about 30 minutes, depending on humidity of kitchen.

5. BAKE—Preheat oven to 325 degrees. Place one cookie sheet in oven and reduce temperature to 300 degrees. Set timer for 7 minutes. Rotate pan. Cook another 6 minutes or until macarons are cooked through. Allow to cool and then remove.

Gourmet French Macarons

Makes
16-20

Frankenstein's monster

sandwiched macarons

FRANKENSTEIN'S MONSTERS

This is one of my favorite designs in the whole book! I love how the brown jimmy sprinkles look like hair and how all the candy elements add such cute details!

Additional
Materials Needed

green food dye

toothpicks

brown mini M&M's

brown Candy Melts

brown jimmy sprinkles

wax paper

royal icing (page 29)

candy eyes

black and green
edible-ink pens

Filling Recommendation:

Shown here with milk chocolate
ganache (page 212).

LEVEL OF DIFFICULTY:
Advanced

Directions

1. PRINT TEMPLATE—Frankenstein's Monster.

2. MIX SHELL BATTER—1 recipe basic macarons (page 14) colored green.

3. PIPE—Pipe a square shape, following the template. Use toothpicks to encourage the batter into the corners.

4. REST—at room temperature for about 30 minutes, depending on humidity of kitchen.

5. BAKE—Preheat oven to 350 degrees. Place one cookie sheet in oven and reduce temperature to 300 degrees. Set timer for 5 minutes. Rotate pan. Cook another 5 minutes or until macarons are cooked through. Allow to cool and then remove.

6. DECORATE—Fill macaron and place brown mini M&M's to represent the bolts. Place in the fridge to chill. Melt brown candy coating. Remove chilled macarons and dip the tops into melted candy coating and then into brown jimmy sprinkles. Place on wax paper and allow to set. Use a dab of royal icing to adhere candy eyes in place. Use edible-ink pens to draw the mouth and stitches.

Gourmet French Macarons

Makes
20–24

SPIDERS

A simple design that is perfect for any Halloween party!

Additional
Materials Needed

black food dye

black licorice rope

royal icing (page 29)

candy eyes

Filling Recommendation:

Shown here with
vanilla buttercream (page 206).

LEVEL OF DIFFICULTY:
Easy

Directions

1. PRINT TEMPLATE—Circle: 1½-inch.

2. MIX SHELL BATTER—1 recipe basic macarons (page 14) colored black.

3. PIPE—Basic circle macarons.

4. REST—at room temperature for about 30 minutes, depending on humidity of kitchen.

5. BAKE—Preheat oven to 350 degrees. Place one cookie sheet in oven and reduce temperature to 300 degrees. Set timer for 5 minutes. Rotate pan. Cook another 5 minutes or until macarons are cooked through. Allow to cool and then remove.

6. DECORATE—Cut licorice rope into 1½-inch pieces. Fill paired macaron shells and place three licorice pieces into the filling on each side to represent the spider legs. Use royal icing to adhere the candy eyes.

Gourmet French Macarons

spooky
bat

Makes
20–24

sandwiched
macarons

SPOOKY BATS

Additional
Materials Needed

black food dye

black Candy Melts

royal icing (page 29)

candy eyes

Filling Recommendation:

Shown here with
vanilla buttercream (page 206).

LEVEL OF DIFFICULTY:
Easy

Directions

1. PRINT TEMPLATE—Circle: 1½-inch.

2. MIX SHELL BATTER—1 recipe basic macarons (page 14) colored black.

3. PIPE—Basic circle macarons.

4. REST—at room temperature for about 30 minutes, depending on humidity of kitchen.

5. BAKE—Preheat oven to 350 degrees. Place one cookie sheet in oven and reduce temperature to 300 degrees. Set timer for 5 minutes. Rotate pan. Cook another 5 minutes or until macarons are cooked through. Allow to cool and then remove.

6. DECORATE—Melt black candy coating in plastic bag. Draw bat wings on paper and cover with wax paper. Cut corner of plastic bag and pipe melted candy coating to fill in wing outline. Set aside to cool. Fill paired macaron shells and place cooled bat wings into the filling on each side. Use royal icing to adhere the candy eyes.

Gourmet French Macarons

black cat

Makes
20-24

sandwiched
macarons

BLACK CATS

Additional
Materials Needed

black food dye

toothpicks

black edible-ink pen

green mini M&M's

orange heart sprinkles

royal icing (page 29)

Filling Recommendation:
Shown here with
vanilla buttercream (page 206).

LEVEL OF DIFFICULTY:
Intermediate

Directions

1. PRINT TEMPLATE—Circle: 1½-inch.

2. MIX SHELL BATTER—1 recipe basic macarons (page 14) colored black.

3. PIPE—Start by piping a basic circle macaron. To add the ears, pipe a small dollop of batter on each side of the circle. Use a toothpick to maneuver the batter into a triangle shape and upward off the parchment at the tip.

4. REST—at room temperature for about 30 minutes, depending on humidity of kitchen.

5. BAKE—Preheat oven to 350 degrees. Place one cookie sheet in oven and reduce temperature to 300 degrees. Set timer for 5 minutes. Rotate pan. Cook another 5 minutes or until macarons are cooked through. Allow to cool and then remove.

6. DECORATE—Use the black edible-ink pen to make a cat eye shape on the green M&M's. Adhere eyes and orange heart nose to the shell using royal icing. Continue with the icing to pipe triangles in the ears and whiskers.

Gourmet French Macarons

WITCH HATS

Additional Materials Needed

black food dye

toothpicks

green Twizzlers Pull-n-Peel

Filling Recommendation:

Shown here with candy corn buttercream (page 227).

LEVEL OF DIFFICULTY: *Easy*

Directions

1. PRINT TEMPLATE—Witch Hat.

2. MIX SHELL BATTER—1 recipe basic macarons (page 14) colored black.

3. PIPE—Start by piping the oval base of the hat. Then pipe upward, reducing pressure on the piping bag as you near the tip. Use a toothpick to maneuver the batter into the top of the hat upward off the parchment at the tip.

4. REST—at room temperature for about 30 minutes, depending on humidity of kitchen.

5. BAKE—Preheat oven to 350 degrees. Place one cookie sheet in oven and reduce temperature to 300 degrees. Set timer for 6 minutes. Rotate pan. Cook another 5 minutes or until macarons are cooked through. Allow to cool and then remove.

6. DECORATE—Cut Twizzlers into 3-inch pieces. Wrap the candy around the hat and secure with filling. Pipe the remainder of the filling and press shells together. Chill in refrigerator to set.

Gourmet French Macarons

MUMMIES

Additional
Materials Needed

white Candy Melts

candy eyes

Filling Recommendation:
Shown here with
chocolate buttercream
(page 206).

LEVEL OF DIFFICULTY:
Easy

Directions

1. PRINT TEMPLATE—Circle: 1½-inch.

2. MIX SHELL BATTER—1 recipe basic macarons (page 14) uncolored.

3. PIPE—Basic circle macarons.

4. REST—at room temperature for about 30 minutes, depending on humidity of kitchen.

5. BAKE—Preheat oven to 350 degrees. Place one cookie sheet in oven and reduce temperature to 300 degrees. Set timer for 6 minutes. Rotate pan. Cook another 5 minutes or until macarons are cooked through. Allow to cool and then remove.

6. DECORATE—Fill and pair macarons. Melt white candy coating in plastic bag. Cut the corner of the plastic bag and pipe melted candy coating across the top of the macarons to resemble mummy wrappings. Stop partway through and adhere eyes to candy coating and then finish piping.

Gourmet French Macarons

haunting gravestone

Makes 18-20

sandwiched macarons

HAUNTING GRAVESTONES

This is a fun way to present macarons at any Halloween event!

Additional Materials Needed

black and green food dye

toothpicks

royal icing (page 29)

shredded coconut

crushed chocolate cookies

Filling Recommendation:

Shown here with
cookies 'n cream filling
(page 231).

Directions

1. PRINT TEMPLATE—Gravestone.

2. MIX SHELL BATTER—1 recipe basic macarons (page 14) colored black.

3. PIPE—Start at the top as if piping a basic circle macaron. Pipe downward to the bottom. Use toothpicks to maneuver batter into corners as much as possible.

4. REST—at room temperature for about 30 minutes, depending on humidity of kitchen.

5. BAKE—Preheat oven to 350 degrees. Place one cookie sheet in oven and reduce temperature to 300 degrees. Set timer for 6 minutes. Rotate pan. Cook another 5 minutes or until macarons are cooked through. Allow to cool and then remove.

6. DECORATE— Use royal icing to pipe decorations on the gravestones. To present, place shredded coconut in a plastic bag with a few drops of green food dye. Shake the bag to coat. Mix this with crushed cookies on a platter to create a graveyard scene. Stand macarons on end to represent graves.

Gourmet French Macarons

PUMPKIN PATCH

These pumpkin macarons are the pick of the patch!

Additional
Materials Needed

orange food dye

brown Candy Melts

wax paper

Filling Recommendation:

Shown here with
pumpkin pie filling (page 223).

LEVEL OF DIFFICULTY:
Easy

Directions

1. PRINT TEMPLATE—Pumpkin.

2. MIX SHELL BATTER—1 recipe basic macarons (page 14) or Cinnamon macaron (page 21) colored orange. Slightly undermix the batter to obtain a textured look on your pumpkins.

3. PIPE—Do not pipe the stem, although it *is* on the template.* Start at the top center of the pumpkin, right under the stem. Pipe outward and down, creating a crescent shape. Without lifting your tip, pipe back up to the top just inside the piped batter. Repeat this process all the way across the pumpkin to create curved vertical lines.

4. REST—at room temperature for about 30 minutes, depending on humidity of kitchen.

5. BAKE—Preheat oven to 350 degrees. Place one cookie sheet in oven and reduce temperature to 300 degrees. Set timer for 6 minutes. Rotate pan. Cook another 5 minutes or until macarons are cooked through. Allow to cool and then remove.

6. DECORATE—Melt brown candy coating in plastic bag. Draw stems on paper and cover with wax paper. Cut corner of plastic bag and pipe melted candy coating to fill in stem outline. Set aside to cool. Fill paired macaron shells and place cooled stems into the filling on the top.

* *If you would like to pipe the stem instead of using candy melts, just separate out a small bit of batter, color it brown, and pipe the stems as well.*

Gourmet French Macarons

AUTUMN LEAVES

These two colorful autumn leaf designs can be made in any beautiful fall color!

Additional Materials Needed

red food dye

toothpicks

brown Candy Melts

wax paper

black and red
edible-ink pens

Filling Recommendation:

Shown here with milk chocolate ganache (page 212).

Other seasonal flavors such as orange-cranberry (page 222), pumpkin pie (page 223), maple pecan (page 224), or snicker-doodle (page 233) would be great as well.

LEVEL OF DIFFICULTY:
Intermediate

Directions

1. PRINT TEMPLATES—Oak Leaf and Simple Leaf.

2. MIX SHELL BATTER—½ recipe basic macarons (page 14) colored red and ½ recipe chocolate macarons (page 20).

3. PIPE—To pipe the oak leaf, start at the top, piping the edge of each curve and working your way around the leaf. Do not pipe the stem, but continue around the leaf until you are back at the top. Fill in any remaining space in the middle.

To pipe the simple leaf, start at the base of the leaf where it is broadest. Move upward, reducing pressure as you reach the tip. Use a toothpick to pull the batter into the point and upward off the parchment at the tip.

4. REST—at room temperature for about 30 minutes, depending on humidity of kitchen.

5. BAKE—Preheat oven to 325 degrees. Place one cookie sheet in oven and reduce temperature to 300 degrees. Set timer for 6 minutes.* Rotate pan. Cook another 5 minutes* or until macarons are cooked through. Allow to cool and then remove.

6. DECORATE—Melt brown candy coating in plastic bag. Draw stems on paper and cover with wax paper. Cut corner of plastic bag and pipe melted candy coating to fill in stem outline. Set aside to cool. Fill paired macaron shells and place cooled stems into the filling on the bottom. Use edible-ink pens to draw the veins through the leaf.

* *Add one minute for chocolate macarons.*

115

Gourmet French Macarons

TURKEYS

Gobble, gobble! These turkey macarons are sure to bring a little something extra to your holiday dessert table!

Additional Materials Needed

black edible-ink pen

white confetti sprinkles

royal icing (page 29)

orange, yellow, and red Starburst*

red writing gel icing

wax paper

rolling pin

small leaf cookie cutter

knife

You could also use AirHeads or fondant.

Filling Recommendation:

Shown here with vanilla buttercream (page 206).

LEVEL OF DIFFICULTY: *Advanced*

Directions

1. PRINT TEMPLATES—Circle: 1 inch, and Circle: 2 inch.

2. MIX SHELL BATTER—1 recipe chocolate macaron (page 20).

3. PIPE—Use the two templates and pipe basic circles. For every two 2-inch circles, pipe one 1-inch circle.

4. REST—at room temperature for about 30 minutes, depending on humidity of kitchen.

5. BAKE—Preheat oven to 350 degrees. Place 1-inch macarons in oven and reduce temperature to 300 degrees. Set timer for 5 minutes. Rotate pan. Cook another 4 minutes or until macarons are cooked through. Set oven to 325 degrees. Place 2-inch macarons in oven and reduce temperature to 300 degrees. Set timer for 8 minutes. Rotate pan. Cook another 7 minutes or until macarons are cooked through. Allow to cool and then remove.

6. DECORATE—Use the edible-ink pen to make an eye on the white confetti sprinkles. Attach to the 1-inch macaron using royal icing. Place an orange Starburst between two sheets of wax paper. Roll it flat with a rolling pin and remove from the wax paper. Cut it into small triangles for the beak. Place a small line of red writing gel icing on the turkey face and attach the beak on top. Set aside and allow to dry. Roll the red, yellow, and orange Starburst that remain in a similar fashion so they are flat. Use a small leaf cookie cutter and cut out feather shapes. Using a knife, make feather imprints on the Starburst. Pair up similar shells to fill. With the flat side of the macaron shell facing up, line up Starburst feathers to fan out halfway around the shell. Pipe filling overtop and seal with the paired shell. Use royal icing to attach the 1-inch macaron face to the turkey body.

Gourmet French Macarons

THANKSGIVING PIE SLICES

Apple, pumpkin, cherry, and pecan—how will you choose?
Since these all use the same pie template, you won't have to!

Additional Materials Needed

orange and brown food dyes

toothpicks

cinnamon

red food gel

paintbrush

Filling Recommendation:

Each pie has a coordinating filling. They are shown here with cherry buttercream (page 219), pecan pie (page 223), apple pie (page 222), and pumpkin pie (page 223).

LEVEL OF DIFFICULTY:
Intermediate

Directions

1. PRINT TEMPLATE—Thanksgiving Pie Slice.

2. MIX SHELL BATTER—1 recipe basic macarons (page 14) or cinnamon macaron (page 21) colored ¾ tan and the rest split and colored orange and brown.

3. PIPE— Before piping, be sure that you have a coupler on the tan piping bag. You will need to switch tips to pipe the tan details. Start with the larger tip. When looking at the template, the plain triangles will be the bottom shell, and the triangles with rectangular tops will be the top shell. The rectangles represent the crust of the pie.

For the apple pie—Pipe triangles for the top and bottom shell tan. Use toothpicks to encourage the batter into the points. Switch to a smaller round tip and pipe zigzag lines to fill the rectangles on the top shell. Sprinkle these with a touch of cinnamon as well.

For the pumpkin pie—Pipe the triangles for the bottom shell tan. Pipe the triangles for the top shell orange. Switch to a smaller round tip and pipe zigzag lines to fill the rectangles on the top shell. Sprinkle these with a touch of cinnamon as well.

For the pecan pie—Pipe the triangles for the bottom shell tan. Pipe the triangles for the top shell brown. Switch to a smaller round tip and pipe zigzag lines to fill the rectangles on the top shell.

For the cherry pie—Pipe all of the triangles tan. Switch to a smaller round tip and pipe zigzag lines to fill the rectangles on the top shell. Then, pipe crossing lines across the top to make a patterned lattice. There will not be any red until the cherry pie is decorated.

(Continued on next page.)

119

Directions (continued)

4. REST—at room temperature for about 30 minutes, depending on humidity of kitchen.

5. BAKE—Preheat oven to 325 degrees. Place one cookie sheet in oven and reduce temperature to 300 degrees. Set timer for 6 minutes. Rotate pan. Cook another 5 minutes or until macarons are cooked through. Allow to cool and then remove.

6. DECORATE—To decorate the pecan pie, top with a whole pecan from the pie filling recipe (page 223). To decorate the cherry pie, use a dry paintbrush to paint on the red food gel between the lattice.

CHRISTMAS TREES

Create a simple tree using sprinkles and a little royal icing!

Additional Materials Needed

· brown and green
food dyes

toothpicks

royal icing (page 29)

red confetti sprinkles

yellow star sprinkles

Filling Recommendation:

Shown here with
vanilla buttercream (page 206),
but many of the seasonal fillings
(page 222–28) would
be great too.

LEVEL OF DIFFICULTY:
Intermediate

Directions

1. PRINT TEMPLATE—Christmas Tree.

2. MIX SHELL BATTER—1 recipe basic macarons (page 14) mostly colored green with a small amount separated and colored brown.

3. PIPE—Start at the top of the tree and pipe downward, filling the triangle from side to side as you go. Use a toothpick to encourage the batter into the corners and to form straight edges. Pipe the rectangle base using the brown batter.

4. REST—at room temperature for about 30 minutes, depending on humidity of kitchen.

5. BAKE—Preheat oven to 325 degrees. Place one cookie sheet in oven and reduce temperature to 300 degrees. Set timer for 7 minutes. Rotate pan. Cook another 7 minutes or until macarons are cooked through. Allow to cool and then remove.

6. DECORATE—Fill paired macarons before decorating. Using the royal icing, make sweeping lines from side to side to represent the garland. Then use the icing to attach red confetti sprinkles as ornaments and a yellow star sprinkle at the top.

Gourmet French Macarons

MINT CANDY CANES

Alternate red and white batter for a classic candy cane macaron!

Additional
Materials Needed

red food dye

toothpicks

Filling Recommendation:

Shown here with
mint butter ream (page 209).

LEVEL OF DIFFICULTY:
Intermediate

Directions

1. PRINT TEMPLATE—Candy Cane.

2. MIX SHELL BATTER—½ recipe basic macarons (page 14) colored red* and ½ recipe basic macarons uncolored.

3. PIPE—Start with the white color at the curved tip of the candy cane. Pipe each white section. Then pick up the red batter and pipe the red sections. Use a toothpick to encourage the batter to meet on the edges, to keep it as straight as possible. Since a candy cane is not a symmetrical shape, be sure you pipe the same number facing each direction.

4. REST—at room temperature for about 30 minutes, depending on humidity of kitchen.

5. BAKE—Preheat oven to 325 degrees. Place one cookie sheet in oven and reduce temperature to 300 degrees. Set timer for 6 minutes. Rotate pan. Cook another 5 minutes or until macarons are cooked through. Allow to cool and then remove.

* Red is a difficult color to achieve, so I recommend splitting the batter from the start to have maximum control over the end result.

Gourmet French Macarons

RUDOLPH THE RED-NOSED REINDEERS

Rudolph has a special place in my heart. It is my mother's maiden name, and I can't help but think about my grandparents and relatives I love so much! This book just wouldn't be complete without this special reindeer!

Additional Materials Needed

brown Candy Melts

wax paper

royal icing (page 29)

mini chocolate chips

red M&M's*

Filling Recommendation:

Shown here with chocolate buttercream (page 206).

LEVEL OF DIFFICULTY:
Easy

Directions

1. PRINT TEMPLATE—Circle: 1½-inch.

2. MIX SHELL BATTER—1 recipe chocolate macarons (page 20).

3. PIPE—Basic circle macarons.

4. REST—at room temperature for about 30 minutes, depending on humidity of kitchen.

5. BAKE—Preheat oven to 350 degrees. Place one cookie sheet in oven and reduce temperature to 300 degrees. Set timer for 6 minutes. Rotate pan. Cook another 6 minutes or until macarons are cooked through. Allow to cool and then remove.

6. DECORATE—Melt brown candy coating in plastic bag. Draw antlers on paper and cover with wax paper. Cut corner of plastic bag and pipe melted candy coating to fill in antler outline. Set aside to cool. For the face, use royal icing to adhere mini chocolate chips as eyes, and a red M&M as a nose. Fill paired macaron shells and place cooled antlers into the filling on each side.

The macarons shown here have a red macaron nose. I happened to have some red batter on hand so I piped small dots of it instead of using red M&M's. Either will work just great for that classic red nose!

Gourmet French Macarons

SNOWMEN

These may seem tricky, but it's all in the presentation!
Stack three different-sized macarons to achieve this snowman design!

Additional Materials Needed

chocolate Candy Melts

mini marshmallows

mini chocolate crème cookies

wax paper

royal icing (page 29)

black sugar pearls

orange Starbust, AirHead, or fondant

Fruit by the Foot or Fruit Roll-Ups

pretzel sticks

Filling Recommendation:

Shown here with coconut Swiss meringue (page 211).

LEVEL OF DIFFICULTY:
*Easy**

Directions

1. PRINT TEMPLATE—Circle: 1½-inch, Circle: 2-inch, Circle: 2½-inch.

2. MIX SHELL BATTER—1 recipe uncolored basic macarons (page 14).

3. PIPE—Basic circle macarons for each template size. Make sure each template is on a different sheet pan because they will each require a different baking times and temperatures.

4. REST—at room temperature for about 30 minutes, depending on humidity of kitchen.

5. BAKE—Bake each size macaron and each tray separate.

For the 1½-inch macarons—Preheat oven to 350 degrees. Place one cookie sheet in oven and reduce temperature to 300 degrees. Set timer for 5 minutes. Rotate pan. Cook another 5 minutes or until macarons are cooked through. Allow to cool and then remove.

For the 2-inch macarons—Preheat oven to 325 degrees. Place one cookie sheet in oven and reduce temperature to 300 degrees. Set timer for 6 minutes. Rotate pan. Cook another 6 minutes or until macarons are cooked through. Allow to cool and then remove.

(Continued on next page.)

*While the macarons are easy, the display is intermediate.

Gourmet French Macarons

129

Directions (continued)

For the 2½-inch macarons—Preheat oven to 325 degrees. Place one cookie sheet in oven and reduce temperature to 275 degrees. Set timer for 7 minutes. Rotate pan. Cook another 7 minutes or until macarons are cooked through. Allow to cool and then remove.

6. DECORATE—Begin making the hats for your snowmen by melting the chocolate candy coating. Dip a mini marshmallow in the melted candy and adhere to the top of a mini chocolate crème cookie. Then coat the entire cookie and marshmallow in candy coating. Set on wax paper to cool. Use royal icing to adhere the black sugar pearls as eyes and a mouth on filled 1½-inch macarons. Roll and shape orange candy or fondant into a carrot shape for the nose and adhere with royal icing. Once the chocolate hat has cooled, adhere to the top of the 1½- inch macarons. Cut the Fruit by the Foot into 4-inch strips and drape over the 2-inch macarons for the scarf. Place two pretzel sticks in the filling of the 2-inch macarons as arms.

To present—Place filled 2½-inch macarons in a row along the bottom of platter. Next, put a row of 2-inch macarons with the arms and scarves. And finally top each snowman off with the 1½-inch macaron faces.

STOCKINGS

Although you can't fill these stockings with toys on Christmas morning,
you *can* fill them with your favorite seasonal flavors (pages 222–28).

Additional
Materials Needed

red and green food dyes

Filling Recommendation:

Shown here with
vanilla buttercream (page 206).

LEVEL OF DIFFICULTY:
Easy

Directions

1. PRINT TEMPLATE—Stocking.

2. MIX SHELL BATTER—½ recipe basic macarons (page 14) colored red.* Also, ½ recipe basic macarons divided and colored mostly green, with a small amount left uncolored.

3. PIPE—Since the stockings are not symmetrical, be sure you pipe the same number facing each direction. Start with either the red or green and pipe the sock portion first. Use minimal pressure in the toe and work upward, increasing pressure through the heel and then reducing pressure again as you move upward. Finish along the top with a band of white batter.

4. REST—at room temperature for about 30 minutes, depending on humidity of kitchen.

5. BAKE—Preheat oven to 325 degrees. Place one cookie sheet in oven and reduce temperature to 300 degrees. Set timer for 6 minutes. Rotate pan. Cook another 5 minutes or until macarons are cooked through. Allow to cool and then remove.

6. DECORATE—Although it is not shown here, adding some beautiful white sanding sugar or sugar crystals would give the top of the stocking great texture! Use a damp brush to wet the shell and then sprinkle on the sugar.

* Red is a difficult color to achieve, so I recommend dividing the batter from the start to have maximum control over the end result.

133

Gourmet French Macarons

gingerbread
man

Makes
10–12

sandwiched
macarons

GINGERBREAD MEN

Additional
Materials Needed

royal icing (page 29)

confetti sprinkles

Filling Recommendation:

Gingerbread filling (page 226).

Directions

1. PRINT TEMPLATE—Gingerbread Man.

2. MIX SHELL BATTER—1 recipe chocolate macarons (page 20).

3. PIPE—Start by piping a basic circle for the head of the gingerbread man. Pick up your tip and pipe across for the two arms. Then pipe each half of the lower body, starting at the foot and moving upward.

4. REST—at room temperature for about 30 minutes, depending on humidity of kitchen.

5. BAKE—Preheat oven to 325 degrees. Place one cookie sheet in oven and reduce temperature to 300 degrees. Set timer for 7 minutes. Rotate pan. Cook another 7 minutes or until macarons are cooked through. Allow to cool and then remove.

6. DECORATE—Use royal icing to add a face and outline of clothes. Add confetti sprinkles for a bow tie or as buttons.

LEVEL OF DIFFICULTY:
Easy

SANTA HATS

Additional
Materials Needed

red food dye

toothpicks

Filling Recommendation:
Shown here with
chocolate buttercream
(page 206).

LEVEL OF DIFFICULTY:
Easy

Directions

1. PRINT TEMPLATE—Santa Hat

2. MIX SHELL BATTER—½ recipe basic macarons (page 14) colored red* and ½ recipe basic macarons uncolored.

3. PIPE—Since the Santa hat is not a symmetrical shape, be sure to pipe the same number facing each direction. Begin by piping the red portion of the hat. Pipe the base and work upward to the tip. Only pipe a small amount of batter in the part of the hat that flops over because you want to be sure it does not spread into the rest of the hat. Use a toothpick if needed to maneuver batter. Pipe the white base of the hat and then pipe a small circle at the top of the hat. Be sure to allow enough space that when the different-colored batters spread, they will not run into each other.

4. REST—at room temperature for about 30 minutes, depending on humidity of kitchen.

5. BAKE—Preheat oven to 325 degrees. Place one cookie sheet in oven and reduce temperature to 300 degrees. Set timer for 7 minutes. Rotate pan. Cook another 6 minutes or until macarons are cooked through. Allow to cool and then remove.

* Red is a difficult color to achieve, so I recommend dividing the batter from the start to have maximum control over the end result.

Gourmet French Macarons

snowflake

Makes
20–24

sandwiched
macarons

WINTER SNOWFLAKES

These are the perfect addition to a wintry day!

Additional
Materials Needed

blue food dye

royal icing (page 29)

Filling Recommendation:

Shown here with
salted caramel buttercream
(page 200) with a salted caramel
sauce (page 237) center.

LEVEL OF DIFFICULTY:
Easy

Directions

1. PRINT TEMPLATE—Circle: 1½-inch.

2. MIX SHELL BATTER—1 recipe basic macarons (page 14) colored light blue.

3. PIPE—Basic circle macarons.

4. REST—at room temperature for about 30 minutes, depending on humidity of kitchen.

5. BAKE—Preheat oven to 350 degrees. Place one cookie sheet in oven and reduce temperature to 300 degrees. Set timer for 5 minutes. Rotate pan. Cook another 5 minutes or until macarons are cooked through. Allow to cool and then remove.

6. DECORATE—Pair and fill your macarons. Then use royal icing to make beautiful snowflake designs on the top shell.

139

Gourmet French Macarons

Sports MACARONS

Show your support for your favorite team with these fun sports-inspired macarons! You can make macarons to resemble sports equipment, macarons to spell out your favorite team name or mascot, or simple macarons with the team's colors.

ball

sandwiched macarons

SOCCER BALLS, BASEBALLS & BASKETBALLS

Perfect for an end-of-the-season or birthday party!

Additional
Materials Needed

orange food dye

black and red
writing gel*

toothpicks

*You could also use edible-ink
pens and draw these patterns
directly on the shell.

Filling Recommendation:

Shown here with vanilla Swiss
meringue (page 210) and dark
chocolate ganache (page 212).

LEVEL OF DIFFICULTY:
*Easy & Intermediate**

Directions

1. PRINT TEMPLATE—Circle: 1½-inch.

2. MIX SHELL BATTER—1 recipe basic macarons (page 14) divided with ⅓ colored orange and the other ⅔ uncolored.

3. PIPE—Basic circle macarons.

4. REST at room temperature for about 30 minutes, depending on humidity of kitchen.

5. BAKE—Preheat oven to 350 degrees. Place one cookie sheet in oven and reduce temperature to 300 degrees. Set timer for 5 minutes. Rotate pan. Cook another 5 minutes or until macarons are cooked through. Allow to cool and then remove.

6. DECORATE—Fill and chill macarons before decorating.

For the basketball and soccer ball—Use the black writing gel to draw each respective pattern. It is helpful to have a picture to use as reference.

For the baseball—Use the red writing gel to pipe a line down each side of the macaron. Take a toothpick and pull the gel into lines coming off the sides to make it look like stitching.

** Basketball and Baseball: Easy. Soccer ball: Intermediate.

143

Gourmet French Macarons

football
Makes
16–20
sandwiched
macarons

and 20–24 team color macarons.

LET'S PLAY SOME FOOTBALL

One of my husband's favorite sports and favorite flavors!

Additional
Materials Needed

food dye to match
team colors

royal icing (page 29)

Filling Recommendation:

Football macarons shown here
with Snickers filling (page 231).

Team color macarons shown
with vanilla buttercream (page
206) and lemon buttercream
(page 208).

LEVEL OF DIFFICULTY:
Easy

Directions

1. PRINT TEMPLATE—Football, Circle: 1½-inch.

2. MIX SHELL BATTER—1 recipe chocolate macarons (page 20) and 1 recipe basic macarons (page 14) divided and colored to match team colors.

3. PIPE—First, pipe basic circles for your team color macarons. Use the chocolate batter to pipe the footballs. Start on one end and increase pressure as you move across horizontally to the middle. Then reduce pressure on the bag as you near the other end.

4. REST—at room temperature for about 30 minutes, depending on humidity of kitchen.

5. BAKE:

For the football macarons—Preheat oven to 325 degrees. Place one cookie sheet in oven and reduce temperature to 300 degrees. Set timer for 7 minutes. Rotate pan. Cook another 7 minutes or until macarons are cooked through. Allow to cool and then remove.

For the circle macarons—Preheat oven to 350 degrees. Place one cookie sheet in oven and reduce temperature to 300 degrees. Set timer for 5 minutes. Rotate pan. Cook another 5 minutes or until macarons are cooked through. Allow to cool and then remove.

6. DECORATE—Use royal icing to pipe the lacing on the football down the center.

Gourmet French Macarons

Animal
MACARONS

Animals make really cute macarons! Animal faces are easy to pipe because they usually only require adding ears. Change the color and add a little candy decoration and you have an adorable animal macaron! The possibilities are endless!

COWS

black food dye

toothpicks

royal icing (page 29)

candy eyes

black sugar pearls

pink Necco Wafers

Filling Recommendation:
I love these with
cookies 'n cream filling
(page 231).

Directions

1. PRINT TEMPLATE—Circle: 1½-inch.

2. MIX SHELL BATTER—1 recipe basic macarons (page 14) uncolored with a small amount (about ¹/6) divided out and colored black.

3. PIPE—First, pipe basic circle macarons using white batter. Pipe small ears on either side of the circle. Use the toothpick to maneuver batter into triangles. Then, fit your black batter bag with a smaller round tip. Pipe small amounts of black batter throughout the circle to look like cow spots. Pipe small black triangles in the ears. Again, use a toothpick to maneuver the batter if necessary.

4. REST—at room temperature for about 30 minutes, depending on humidity of kitchen.

5. BAKE—Preheat oven to 350 degrees. Place one cookie sheet in oven and reduce temperature to 300 degrees. Set timer for 6 minutes. Rotate pan. Cook another 5 minutes or until macarons are cooked through. Allow to cool and then remove.

6. DECORATE—Use royal icing to adhere candy eyes to the shell and black sugar pearls in the middle of a pink Necco Wafer for the nose. Use royal icing again to attach the wafer to the shell.

LEVEL OF DIFFICULTY:
Intermediate

149

Gourmet French Macarons

Makes
20–24

sandwiched
macarons

PIGS

Filling Recommendation:
Shown here with marshmallow filling (page 238), although it would be fun to use maple brown sugar & bacon filling (page 241)!

LEVEL OF DIFFICULTY:
Easy

Directions

1. PRINT TEMPLATE—Circle: 1½-inch.

2. MIX SHELL BATTER—1 recipe basic macarons (page 14) colored pink.

3. PIPE—Basic circle macarons.

4. REST—at room temperature for about 30 minutes, depending on humidity of kitchen.

5. BAKE—Preheat oven to 350 degrees. Place one cookie sheet in oven and reduce temperature to 300 degrees. Set timer for 5 minutes. Rotate pan. Cook another 5 minutes or until macarons are cooked through. Allow to cool and then remove.

6. DECORATE—Melt pink candy coating in plastic bag. Draw small ears on paper and cover with wax paper. Cut corner of plastic bag and pipe melted candy coating to fill in the ear outline. Set aside to cool. Fill paired macaron shells and place cooled ears into the filling on the top. Make two lines in the middle of the pink Necco Wafer to represent nostrils. Adhere the wafer and candy eyes to the shell using royal icing.

* You could also pipe ears directly onto the shell using macaron batter instead of candy coating ears.

Gourmet French Macarons

LIONS

These cute wild lions are all in the decorating. Pipe basic circle macarons and transform them in a few simple steps!

Additional
Materials Needed

yellow food dye

royal icing (page 29)

black sugar pearls

brown mini M&M's

brown and/or black
jimmy sprinkles

black edible-ink pen

yellow Candy Melts

wax paper

Filling Recommendation:

Shown here with
dark chocolate ganache
(page 212).

LEVEL OF DIFFICULTY:
Advanced

Directions

1. PRINT TEMPLATE—Circle: 1½-inch.

2. MIX SHELL BATTER—½ recipe basic macarons (page 14) colored yellow.

3. PIPE—Basic circle macarons.

4. REST—at room temperature for about 30 minutes, depending on humidity of kitchen.

5. BAKE—Preheat oven to 350 degrees. Place one cookie sheet in oven and reduce temperature to 300 degrees. Set timer for 5 minutes. Rotate pan. Cook another 5 minutes or until macarons are cooked through. Allow to cool and then remove.

6. DECORATE—Use royal icing to adhere the black sugar pearl eyes and pipe the cheeks. While still wet, add the M&M for a nose and jimmy sprinkles as whiskers. Draw a small mouth under the nose using a black edible-ink pen. Melt yellow candy coating in an unzipped plastic bag. Draw an outline of the ray/mane shape on a piece of paper. Be sure that the inside circle is smaller than the macaron shells so that it can be sandwiched in the middle by them. Place wax paper over drawing, snip the corner of the plastic bag and pipe melted candy over the drawing. Allow to cool and remove from wax paper. Place between shells and then fill. The filling will help to keep the mane in place.

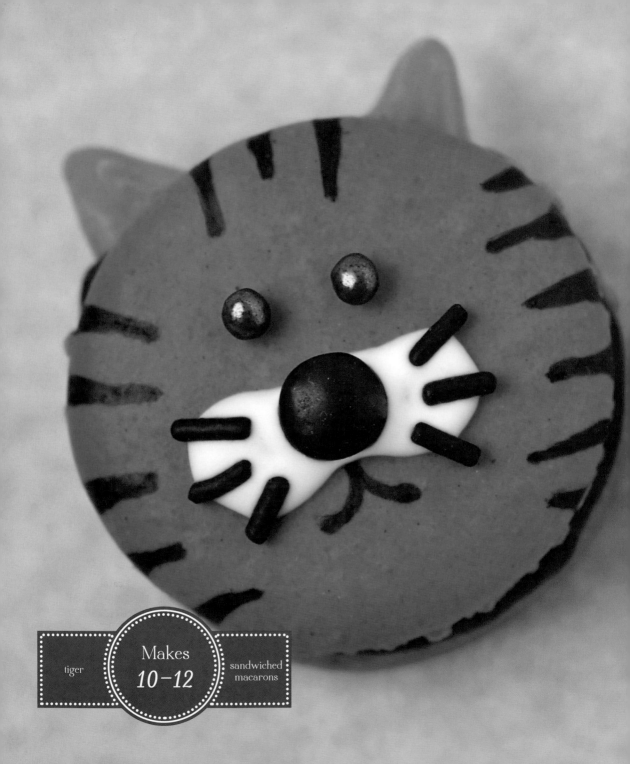

TIGERS

These cute wild tigers are all in the decorating. Pipe basic circle
macarons and transform them in a few simple steps!

Additional Materials Needed

orange food dye

royal icing (page 29)

black sugar pearls

brown mini M&M's

black edible-ink pen

brown and/or black
jimmy sprinkles

orange Candy Melts

wax paper

Filling Recommendation:

Shown here with
dark chocolate ganache
(page 212).

LEVEL OF DIFFICULTY:
Advanced

Directions

1. PRINT TEMPLATE—Circle: 1½-inch.

2. MIX SHELL BATTER—½ recipe basic macarons (page 14)
colored orange.

3. PIPE—Basic circle macarons.

4. REST—at room temperature for about 30 minutes, depending
on humidity of kitchen.

5. BAKE—Preheat oven to 350 degrees. Place one cookie sheet in
oven and reduce temperature to 300 degrees. Set timer for 5 minutes.
Rotate pan. Cook another 5 minutes or until macarons are cooked
through. Allow to cool and then remove.

6. DECORATE—Use royal icing to adhere the black sugar pearl
eyes and pipe the cheeks. While still wet—add the M&M for a nose,
and jimmy sprinkles as whiskers. Draw a small mouth under the nose
using a black edible-ink pen. Melt orange candy coating in a plastic
bag. Draw small ears on paper and cover with wax paper. Cut corner
of plastic bag and pipe melted candy coating to fill in the ear outline.
Set aside to cool. Fill paired macaron shells and place cooled ears into
the filling on the top. Use the black edible-ink pen to draw stripes
around the perimeter of the shell.

Gourmet French Macarons

FROGS

Additional Materials Needed

green food dye

royal icing (page 29)

candy eyes

black edible-ink pen

Filling Recommendation:
Shown here with marshmallow filling (page 238).

If using pistachio batter, then I recommend the pistachio buttercream (page 207).

LEVEL OF DIFFICULTY.
Easy

Directions

1. PRINT TEMPLATE—Frog.

2. MIX SHELL BATTER—1 recipe basic macarons (page 14) or pistachio macaron (page 21) colored green.

3. PIPE—Start by piping a basic circle macaron for the face. Then pipe a small circle for each eye, following the template.

4. REST—at room temperature for about 30 minutes, depending on humidity of kitchen.

5. BAKE—Preheat oven to 325 degrees. Place one cookie sheet in oven and reduce temperature to 300 degrees. Set timer for 6 minutes. Rotate pan. Cook another 5 minutes or until macarons are cooked through. Allow to cool and then remove.

6. DECORATE—Use royal icing to attach the candy eyes and a black edible-ink pen to draw a silly mouth.

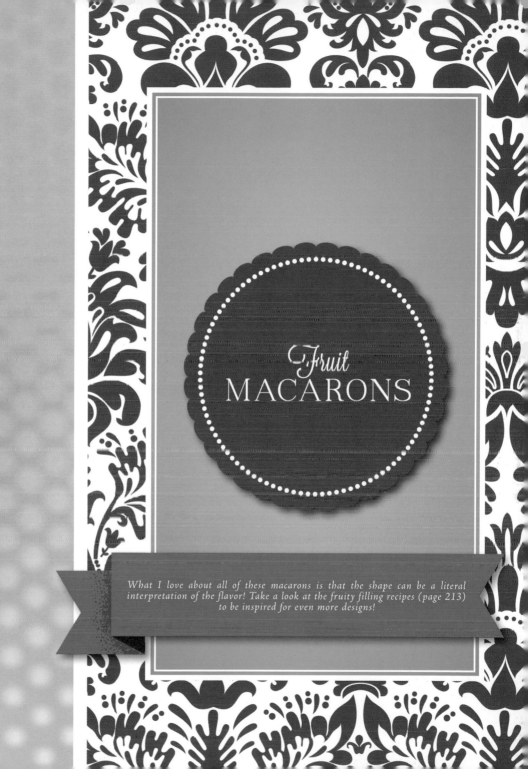

Fruit
MACARONS

What I love about all of these macarons is that the shape can be a literal interpretation of the flavor! Take a look at the fruity filling recipes (page 213) to be inspired for even more designs!

Makes **8–10** (of each) lemon & lime sandwiched macarons

and 6–8 orange macarons

CITRUS: LEMONS, LIMES & ORANGES

Additional
Materials Needed

orange, green, and yellow food dye

toothpicks

Filling Recommendation:

Lemon buttercream (page 208), lemon curd (page 217), lime curd (page 217), and/or orange curd (page 217).

LEVEL OF DIFFICULTY:
Easy

Directions

1. PRINT TEMPLATES—Circle: 2-inch, Lemon.

2. MIX SHELL BATTER—1 recipe basic macarons (page 14) divided evenly and colored yellow, green, and orange.

3. PIPE—Use the orange batter to pipe basic circles on the 2-inch template. Use the green and yellow batter for the lemon template. Pipe from one side to the other, slightly increasing pressure through the middle. Use a toothpick to pull the batter out into the points and upward off the parchment at the tips.

4. REST—at room temperature for about 30 minutes, depending on humidity of kitchen.

5. BAKE—Preheat oven to 325 degrees. Place one cookie sheet in oven and reduce temperature to 300 degrees. Set timer for 6 minutes. Rotate pan. Cook another 5 minutes or until macarons are cooked through. Allow to cool and then remove.

Gourmet French Macarons

BANANAS

yellow food dye

toothpicks

Filling Recommendation:

The Elvis (page 240) or chocolate peanut butter banana filling (page 240).

LEVEL OF DIFFICULTY:
Easy

Directions

1. PRINT TEMPLATE— Banana.

2. MIX SHELL BATTER—1 recipe basic macarons (page 14) colored yellow.

3. PIPE—Since a banana is not a symmetrical shape, be sure you pipe the same number facing each direction according to the templates. Begin at the bottom of the banana and work toward the tip. Increase pressure slightly through the bend of the banana. Pipe a small drop for the tip and use a toothpick to maneuver batter into desired position.

4. REST—at room temperature for about 30 minutes, depending on humidity of kitchen.

5. BAKE—Preheat oven to 325 degrees. Place one cookie sheet in oven and reduce temperature to 300 degrees. Set timer for 5 minutes. Rotate pan. Cook another 5 minutes or until macarons are cooked through. Allow to cool and then remove.

Gourmet French Macarons

Makes 15–20

CHERRIES

Additional
Materials Needed

red food dye

green Candy Melts

wax paper

Filling Recommendation:

Cherry buttercream (page 219)
or chocolate-covered cherry
filling (page 242).

LEVEL OF DIFFICULTY,
Easy

Directions

1. PRINT TEMPLATE—Cherry.

2. MIX SHELL BATTER—1 recipe basic macarons (page 14)
colored red.

3. PIPE—Make two basic circle shapes following the template. As
the batter spreads, these will join in the middle and become one shell.

4. REST—at room temperature for about 30 minutes, depending
on humidity of kitchen.

5. BAKE—Preheat oven to 350 degrees. Place one cookie sheet in
oven and reduce temperature to 300 degrees. Set timer for 5 minutes.
Rotate pan. Cook another 5 minutes or until macarons are cooked
through. Allow to cool and then remove.

6. DECORATE—Melt green candy coating in plastic bag. Draw
joined cherry stems on paper and cover with wax paper. Cut corner of
plastic bag and pipe melted candy coating along the stem outline. Set
aside to cool. Fill paired macaron shells and place cooled stems into
the filling on the top.

Gourmet French Macarons

Makes
14–18

STRAWBERRIES

Additional
Materials Needed

red and green food dye

red edible-ink pen

Filling Recommendation:

Fresh macerated berries (page
214) and vanilla buttercream
(page 206).

LEVEL OF DIFFICULTY:
Easy

Directions

1. PRINT TEMPLATE—Strawberry.

2. MIX SHELL BATTER—1 recipe basic macarons (page 14)
colored ¾ red and ¼ green.

3. PIPE—Pipe the body of the strawberry first, starting at the top
and reducing pressure on the bag as you pipe toward the bottom. Pipe
the green batter at the top for the stems with two or three petals.

4. REST—at room temperature for about 30 minutes, depending
on humidity of kitchen.

5. BAKE—Preheat oven to 325 degrees. Place one cookie sheet in
oven and reduce temperature to 300 degrees. Set timer for 6 minutes.
Rotate pan. Cook another 5 minutes or until macarons are cooked
through. Allow to cool and then remove.

6. DECORATE—Use the red edible-ink pen to draw seeds on the
body of the strawberry.

Birthday
MACARONS

Balloons, cupcakes, and ice cream!
Cute designs inspired by birthday party classics!

BALLOONS

Additional Materials Needed

various colors of food dye*

toothpicks

lollipop sticks

*Use any colors that match your party theme.

Filling Recommendation:

Shown here with vanilla buttercream (page 206).

LEVEL OF DIFFICULTY: *Easy*

Directions

1. PRINT TEMPLATE—Balloon.

2. MIX SHELL BATTER—1 recipe basic macarons (page 14) divided and colored.

3. PIPE—Pipe a basic circle and pull the tip toward the base of the balloon as you finish piping. Pipe a dollop of batter at the end of the balloon and use a toothpick to maneuver batter into place.

4. REST—at room temperature for about 30 minutes, depending on humidity of kitchen.

5. BAKE—Preheat oven to 325 degrees. Place one cookie sheet in oven and reduce temperature to 300 degrees. Set timer for 5 minutes. Rotate pan. Cook another 5 minutes or until macarons are cooked through. Allow to cool and then remove.

6. DECORATE—Fill macarons and place a lollipop in each macaron through the filling. Chill in the refrigerator until it is time for the party. Display using a covered Styrofoam block.

Gourmet French Macarons

CUPCAKES

Additional
Materials Needed

pink food dye

royal icing (page 29)

red, orange,
and yellow nonpareils

Directions

1. PRINT TEMPLATE—Cupcake.

2. MIX SHELL BATTER—1 recipe basic macarons (page 14). Color ½ pink and leave ½ uncolored.

3. PIPE—Pipe the pink base of the cupcake first. Then pipe the top of the cupcake with white batter in three horizontal rows. Pipe across the widest part first that meets the pink base. Pick up your tip and start a new smaller line above that. Finally, pipe a small circle at the top.

4. REST—at room temperature for about 30 minutes, depending on humidity of kitchen.

5. BAKE—Preheat oven to 325 degrees. Place one cookie sheet in oven and reduce temperature to 300 degrees. Set timer for 6 minutes. Rotate pan. Cook another 6 minutes or until macarons are cooked through. Allow to cool and then remove.

6. DECORATE—You will need pink and white royal icing to decorate. Use a small round tip for the pink royal icing and pipe vertical lines on the base of the cupcake to mimic the fold in a cupcake liner. Then pipe white royal icing in a swirling pattern to mimic frosting. Top with different colors of nonpareils.

Filling Recommendation:

Shown here with
cake batter buttercream
(page 236).

LEVEL OF DIFFICULTY:
Advanced

Gourmet French Macarons

Makes
16–20

ice cream
cone

sandwiched
macarons

ICE CREAM CONES

Although you could make these any flavor or color, for this design
I'll describe how to make amazing vanilla ice cream cones with sprinkles!

Additional Materials Needed

brown food dye

toothpicks

multicolored jimmy sprinkles

red Skittles or M&M's

Filling Recommendation:

Shown here with vanilla buttercream (page 206).

LEVEL OF DIFFICULTY: Intermediate

Directions

1. PRINT TEMPLATE—Ice Cream Cone.

2. MIX SHELL BATTER—1 recipe basic macarons (page 14) or vanilla bean macarons (page 20). Leave ⅔ uncolored and color the other ⅓ tan.

3. PIPE—Make the tan cone first by piping from the widest part downward, reducing pressure on your piping bag as you go. Use toothpicks to encourage the batter into the tip. Pipe your white batter in the top half circle of the ice cream. Then lift your tip and pipe small circles across the middle to join the white and tan batter. This will give the bottom of the scoop of ice cream the rounded edges. Before the batter forms a skin, sprinkle multicolored jimmy sprinkles over the ice cream scoop.

4. REST—at room temperature for about 30 minutes, depending on humidity of kitchen.

5. BAKE—Preheat oven to 325 degrees. Place one cookie sheet in oven and reduce temperature to 275 degrees. Set timer for 7 minutes. Rotate pan. Cook another 5 minutes or until macarons are cooked through. Allow to cool and then remove.

6. DECORATE—Fill paired macarons and place a red Skittle or M&M in the filling on top to represent a cherry.

Gourmet French Macarons

ice cream
sandwich

Makes
18-22

sandwiched
macarons

NEAPOLITAN ICE CREAM SANDWICHES

I scream, you scream, we all scream for ice cream! This is one of my favorite ways to eat macarons—filled with ice cream! It is a great solution for overcooked macarons since the ice cream softens them right up!

Additional Materials Needed

pink food dye

pink, brown, and white sprinkles

Filling Recommendation:

Shown here with chocolate, vanilla, and strawberry ice cream.

LEVEL OF DIFFICULTY: *Easy*

Directions

1. PRINT TEMPLATE—Circle: 2-inch.

2. MIX SHELL BATTER—1 recipe basic macarons (page 14) divided evenly into uncolored batter and pink batter. Also, make ½ recipe chocolate macaron (page 20).

3. PIPE—Basic circle macarons.

4. REST—at room temperature for about 30 minutes, depending on humidity of kitchen.

5. BAKE—Preheat oven to 325 degrees. Place one cookie sheet in oven and reduce temperature to 300 degrees. Set timer for 6 minutes. Rotate pan. Cook another 6 minutes or until macarons are cooked through. Add two minutes total time for cooking chocolate macarons. Allow to cool and then remove.

6. DECORATE—Fill with ice cream and roll in colored sprinkles. Place immediately in freezer until ready to serve. Let sit at room temperature about 5 minutes before serving.

Gourmet French Macarons

Wedding Celebration
MACARONS

Macarons are a fast growing trend for weddings!
Use them as dessert or even favors. In this section, I'll share how to present
and decorate classic macarons as well as some fun and detailed unique ones!

wedding cake   Makes 6-8   macarons

WEDDING CAKES

Stack and decorate various sizes of macaron shells to make a wedding cake design!
These would be perfect favors for a bridal shower!

Additional Materials Needed

white sugar pearls

paintbrush

pearl shimmer dust

white fondant flowers

Filling Recommendation.

Shown here with
vanilla buttercream (page 206).

LEVEL OF DIFFICULTY.
Intermediate

Directions

1. PRINT TEMPLATES—Circle: 1-inch, Circle: 1½-inch, Circle: 2-inch, Circle: 2½-inch.

2. MIX SHELL BATTER—1 recipe basic macarons (page 14) uncolored.

3. PIPE—basic circle macarons for each template size. Be sure each template is on a different sheet pan since they will each require a different baking time and temperature. You will not need to pair the macaron shells. Pipe the same number of each size.

4. REST—at room temperature for about 30 minutes, depending on humidity of kitchen.

5. BAKE—Bake each size macaron and each tray separate.

For the 1-inch macarons—Preheat oven to 350 degrees. Place one cookie sheet in oven and reduce temperature to 300 degrees. Set timer for 5 minutes. Rotate pan. Cook another 4 minutes or until macarons are cooked through. Allow to cool and then remove.

For the 1½-inch macarons—Preheat oven to 350 degrees. Place one cookie sheet in oven and reduce temperature to 300 degrees. Set timer for 5 minutes. Rotate pan. Cook another 5 minutes or until macarons are cooked through. Allow to cool and then remove.

(Continued on next page.)

Gourmet French Macarons

For the 2-inch macarons—Preheat oven to 325 degrees. Place one cookie sheet in oven and reduce temperature to 300 degrees. Set timer for 6 minutes. Rotate pan. Cook another 6 minutes or until macarons are cooked through. Allow to cool and then remove.

For the 2½-inch macarons—Preheat oven to 325 degrees. Place one cookie sheet in oven and reduce temperature to 275 degrees. Set timer for 7 minutes. Rotate pan. Cook another 7 minutes or until macarons are cooked through. Allow to cool and then remove.

6. DECORATE—Pipe a generous amount of filling on the flat side of a 2-inch shell and press this down gently onto the rounded part of a 2½-inch shell. Repeat this process for each size shell until you have 4 tiers. Place white sugar pearls along the filling on each tier. Use a paintbrush to apply pearl shimmer dust to fondant flowers for decoration.

Mindy Cone

ENGAGEMENT RINGS

Give your macaron a metallic luster by brushing it with edible shimmering dust!
These would be a fun way to announce your engagement or just to serve at a party!

Additional
Materials Needed

black food dye

paintbrush

silver shimmer dust

white Candy Melts

wax paper

royal icing (page 29)

Filling Recommendation:

Shown here with
vanilla Swiss meringue
(page 210).

LEVEL OF DIFFICULTY:
Intermediate

Directions

1. PRINT TEMPLATE—Circle: 2-inch.

2. MIX SHELL BATTER—1 recipe basic macarons (page 14) colored with a small drop of black food dye for a gray color.

3. PIPE—Using the template as a guide, pipe directly over the line, leaving the center open. Even pressure on your piping bag is key to maintaining a nice circle.

4. REST—at room temperature for about 30 minutes, depending on humidity of kitchen.

5. BAKE—Preheat oven to 350 degrees. Place one cookie sheet in oven and reduce temperature to 300 degrees. Set timer for 4 minutes. Rotate pan. Cook another 4 minutes or until macarons are cooked through. Allow to cool and then remove.

6. DECORATE—Fill macarons. Dip the paintbrush in shimmer dust and cover the entire shell. Melt white candy coating in a plastic bag. Draw a diamond outline on paper (I use a photo for reference) and cover with wax paper. Cut corner of plastic bag and pipe melted candy coating to fill in diamond outline. Once cooled, remove candy diamonds and pipe royal icing to add dimension to the shape. Place diamonds into the filling.

Gourmet French Macarons

OMBRÉ MACARONS

This is a really fun way to display a color scheme at any event!

Additional Materials Needed

food dye (color of choice)

Filling Recommendation:

Shown here with coconut curd (page 216).

Directions

1. PRINT TEMPLATE—Circle: 1½-inch.

2. MIX SHELL BATTER—1 recipe basic macarons (page 14). Separate batter into three different bowls and add varying amounts of food dye to achieve a spectrum of shades.

3. PIPE—Basic circular macarons.

4. REST—at room temperature for about 30 minutes, depending on humidity of kitchen.

5. BAKE—Preheat oven to 350 degrees. Place one cookie sheet in oven and reduce temperature to 300 degrees. Set timer for 5 minutes. Rotate pan. Cook another 5 minutes or until macarons are cooked through. Allow to cool and then remove.

Gourmet French Macarons

Makes
20-24

monogram   sandwiched
                  macarons

MONOGRAMMED MACARONS

Classy and personalized, these monogrammed macarons make great favors!

Additional
Materials Needed

royal icing (page 29)

Filling Recommendation:

Shown here with
chocolate buttercream
(page 206).

LEVEL OF DIFFICULTY:
Easy

Directions

1. PRINT TEMPLATE—Circle: 1½-inch.

2. MIX SHELL BATTER—1 recipe chocolate macaron (page 20).

3. PIPE—Basic circular macarons.

4. REST—at room temperature for about 30 minutes, depending on humidity of kitchen.

5. BAKE—Preheat oven to 350 degrees. Place one cookie sheet in oven and reduce temperature to 300 degrees. Set timer for 6 minutes. Rotate pan. Cook another 6 minutes or until macarons are cooked through. Allow to cool and then remove.

6. DECORATE—Pipe royal icing directly onto the shell in whatever design you want! Shown here piped with an individual letter in the center and a polka-dot outline

Gourmet French Macarons

brushed
icing flower

Makes
20–24

sandwiched
macarons

BRUSHED ICING FLOWERS

Additional
Materials Needed

yellow food dye

royal icing (page 29)

paintbrush

small dish of water

white nonpareils

Filling Recommendation:

Shown here with
lemon buttercream (page 208)
and a lemon curd center
(page 217).

LEVEL OF DIFFICULTY:
Intermediate

Directions

1. PRINT TEMPLATE—Circle: 1½-inch.

2. MIX SHELL BATTER—1 recipe basic macarons (page 14)
colored yellow.

3. PIPE—Basic circular macarons.

4. REST—at room temperature for about 30 minutes, depending
on humidity of kitchen.

5. BAKE—Preheat oven to 350 degrees. Place one cookie sheet in
oven and reduce temperature to 300 degrees. Set timer for 5 minutes.
Rotate pan. Cook another 5 minutes or until macarons are cooked
through. Allow to cool and then remove.

6. DECORATE—Pipe royal icing for
the outline of the flower. Dip a paintbrush
in water and sweep over the icing into the
center of the flower. Repeat all the way
around the flower outline. Add a few white
nonpareils to the center.

Gourmet French Macarons

Baby Shower
MACARONS

Whether it's a boy or a girl, these baby-themed macarons are adorable!
Use them as a gender reveal, at a baby shower, or as a gift for new parents!

baby sandwiched macarons

BABY GIRLS & BOYS

Filling Recommendation:

Shown here with
vanilla buttercream (page 206),
colored pink and blue.

LEVEL OF DIFFICULTY:
Easy

Directions

1. PRINT TEMPLATE—Circle: 1½-inch.

2. MIX SHELL BATTER—1 recipe basic macarons (page 14) colored tan.

3. PIPE—Basic circle macarons.

4. REST—at room temperature for about 30 minutes, depending on humidity of kitchen.

5. BAKE—Preheat oven to 350 degrees. Place one cookie sheet in oven and reduce temperature to 300 degrees. Set timer for 6 minutes. Rotate pan. Cook another 5 minutes or until macarons are cooked through. Allow to cool and then remove.

6. DECORATE—With the black edible-ink pen, draw a baby face directly on the macaron shell. Use royal icing to adhere a single piece of candy necklace as a pacifier. Place a sugar pearl into the opening with additional icing. For the baby girl, use icing to secure two pink hearts together in the shape of a bow. To make the bonnet, fold a cupcake wrapper in half, and use the hole puncher to make holes on each side. Thread string through the holes and tie under the bottom of the shell.

Gourmet French Macarons

BABY BOTTLES

pink, yellow, blue,
and green food dye

royal icing (page 29)

Filling Recommendation:

Shown here with
marshmallow filling (page 238).

LEVEL OF DIFFICULTY:
Intermediate

Directions

1. PRINT TEMPLATE—Baby Bottle.

2. MIX SHELL BATTER—1 recipe basic macarons (page 14) mostly uncolored with a small amount colored pink, blue, yellow, or green to match the desired theme.

3. PIPE—Use the white batter to pipe the main body of the bottle first. Then use the colored batter to pipe a line across the top of the body of the bottle. Pick up the white batter again and pipe a small line and then a small circle to represent the top of the bottle, following the template.

4. REST—at room temperature for about 30 minutes, depending on humidity of kitchen.

5. BAKE Preheat oven to 325 degrees. Place one cookie sheet in oven and reduce temperature to 300 degrees. Set timer for 6 minutes. Rotate pan. Cook another 6 minutes or until macarons are cooked through. Allow to cool and then remove.

6. DECORATE—Using royal icing, pipe horizontal lines on the side of the bottle to represent measurements.

Gourmet French Macarons

Makes
16–20

carriage sandwiched macarons

BABY CARRIAGES

Additional Materials Needed

pink and blue food dyes

toothpicks

royal icing (page 29)

large crystal sugar sprinkles

pink and blue Candy Melts

black edible-ink pen

Filling Recommendation:

Shown here with
vanilla Swiss meringue
(page 210).

LEVEL OF DIFFICULTY: Advanced

Directions

1. PRINT TEMPLATE—Baby Carriage.

2. MIX SHELL BATTER—1 recipe basic macarons (page 14) divided and colored pink and blue.

3. PIPE—Since the carriage is not a symmetrical shape, be sure you pipe the same number facing each direction according to the templates. Pipe from one corner to the other, making a "c" shape. Use toothpicks to encourage the batter into the points of the carriage.

4. REST—at room temperature for about 30 minutes, depending on humidity of kitchen.

5. BAKE—Preheat oven to 325 degrees. Place one cookie sheet in oven and reduce temperature to 300 degrees. Set timer for 6 minutes. Rotate pan. Cook another 5 minutes or until macarons are cooked through. Allow to cool and then remove.

6. DECORATE—Use royal icing to pipe an outline on the carriage and lines on the carriage hood to add dimension to the shape. Sprinkle sugar sprinkles across the top of the carriage for decoration. Write directly on the Candy Melt wafers with a black edible-ink pen to give them spokes so they can represent the wheels of the carriage. Push the wheels into the filling of the macaron along the bottom.

Gourmet French Macarons

baby feet & pacifier

Makes 18–22

sandwiched macarons

BABY FEET IMPRESSIONS & PACIFIERS

Additional
Materials Needed

blue, pink, and/or
yellow food dyes

toothpicks

Filling Recommendation:

Shown here with
vanilla buttercream (page 206).

LEVEL OF DIFFICULTY:
Intermediate

Directions

1. PRINT TEMPLATE—Circle: 1½-inch.

2. MIX SHELL BATTER—1 recipe basic macarons (page 14) divided with a small amount colored pink, blue, and/or yellow to match your desired theme. Leave the rest uncolored.

3. PIPE—Use the uncolored batter and pipe basic circle macarons.

To make the baby feet impressions—Use a small round tip and pipe the bases of the feet first on top of the circle. Then go back and pipe each toe impression. Use a toothpick to maneuver batter into the desired position.

To make the pacifier design—Pipe one color as the base on top of the circle and use a toothpick to maneuver the batter into position. Then use yellow batter to pipe the top of the pacifier shape. I found it helpful to use a photo as visual reference for both the feet and the pacifier.

4. REST—at room temperature for about 30 minutes, depending on humidity of kitchen.

5. BAKE—Preheat oven to 350 degrees. Place one cookie sheet in oven and reduce temperature to 300 degrees. Set timer for 5 minutes. Rotate pan. Cook another 5 minutes or until macarons are cooked through. Allow to cool and then remove.

Gourmet French Macarons

BABY RATTLES

blue, pink, yellow,
and/or green food dyes

white large
crystal sugar sprinkles

striped straws

white ribbon

Filling Recommendation:

Shown here with
vanilla buttercream (page 206).

LEVEL OF DIFFICULTY:
Intermediate

Directions

1. PRINT TEMPLATES—Circle: 2-inch and Circle: 1-inch.

2. MIX SHELL BATTER—1 recipe basic macarons (page 14) divided and colored blue, pink, yellow, and/or green to match your desired theme.

3. PIPE—Be sure to pipe 2-inch and 1-inch basic circle macarons on separate baking sheets since they will require different baking temperatures and times. Pipe the same number of macarons for each size.

4. REST—at room temperature for about 30 minutes, depending on humidity of kitchen.

5. BAKE

For the 1-inch macarons—Preheat oven to 350 degrees. Place one cookie sheet in oven and reduce temperature to 300 degrees. Set timer for 5 minutes. Rotate pan. Cook another 4 minutes or until macarons are cooked through.

For the 2-inch macarons—Preheat oven to 325 degrees. Place one cookie sheet in oven and reduce temperature to 300 degrees. Set timer for 6 minutes. Rotate pan. Cook another 6 minutes or until macarons are cooked through.

6. DECORATE—Pair similar-sized shells and fill. Roll filled macarons through large white sugar crystals so that the filling on the edge catches the sugar. Insert the striped straw into the filling of a 2-inch macaron and a 1-inch macaron on each side. I recommend pressing the straw flat on both ends before inserting it into the filling. Tie a white ribbon bow on the straw.

Gourmet French Macarons

Basic
FILLINGS

Buttercream

BUTTERCREAM IS A GREAT BLANK SLATE for a multitude of flavor profiles. The consistency is perfect for macarons—it holds its shape well but is sticky enough to keep the two shells sandwiched together. I often make a large batch of vanilla buttercream and divide it up to make different flavors. If you are using it the same day, leave it out at room temperature until use. Buttercream will stay fresh for up to two weeks in the fridge and can be frozen in an airtight container. Just be sure to bring it up to room temperature before piping onto your macarons.

• VANILLA BEAN BUTTERCREAM •

1 cup unsalted butter, softened
3½ cups sifted powdered sugar
1½ tsp. vanilla bean paste

1 tsp. almond extract
2 Tbsp. water
¼ tsp. salt

Mix butter and powdered sugar together on low speed. Add vanilla bean paste, almond extract, water, and salt. Mix on high speed until smooth.

• CHOCOLATE BUTTERCREAM •

1 cup unsalted butter, softened
3½ cups sifted powder sugar
1 cup cocoa powder

1½ tsp. almond extract
2 Tbsp. water
¼ tsp. salt

Mix butter and powdered sugar together on low speed. Add cocoa powder and continue to mix on low speed. Add, almond extract, water, and salt. Mix on high speed until smooth.

206

• PISTACHIO BUTTERCREAM •

1 cup unsalted butter, softened
3½ cups sifted powdered sugar
1 tsp. almond extract

2 Tbsp. water
¼ tsp. salt
3 Tbsp. pistachio paste*

Mix butter and powdered sugar together on low speed. Add almond extract, water, and salt. Mix on high speed until smooth. Add pistachio paste to desired taste.**

*NO PISTACHIO PASTE? Place 1 cup of shelled, skinned pistachios in your food processor and pulse to medium-fine consistency. Add to buttercream for desired texture.
Tip: Save any extra for a pistachio macaron shell

**Pistachio paste and grounds will mature over time in the buttercream and increase in strength of flavor.

• PEANUT BUTTER WHIPPED BUTTERCREAM •

2 cups vanilla bean buttercream
   (page 206)

¾ cup creamy peanut butter

Mix ingredients on high until volume increases by 25 percent.

• RASPBERRY BUTTERCREAM •

2 cups vanilla bean buttercream
   (page 206)

½ cup pureed raspberries

Mix buttercream on low and add pureed raspberry slowly—1 tablespoon at a time. When fully incorporated, mix on high for 2 minutes.

The raspberry flavor will enhance as the buttercream matures over time.

207

• LEMON CURD BUTTERCREAM •

2 cups vanilla bean buttercream
   (page 206)

¾ cup lemon curd (page 217)

Mix ingredients on low speed until fully incorporated.

• CREAM CHEESE BUTTERCREAM •

8 oz. cream cheese, room
   temperature
½ cup butter, room temperature

3½ cups powdered sugar
1 tsp. vanilla bean extract

Blend cream cheese and butter together. On low speed, add powdered sugar 1 cup at a time. Add vanilla bean extract and blend on high 2–3 minutes.

• SALTED CARAMEL BUTTERCREAM •

2 cups vanilla bean buttercream
   (page 206)

¾ cup salted caramel sauce
   (page 237)*

Mix on low speed until fully incorporated.

*You can use store-bought.

Mindy Cone

2 cups vanilla bean buttercream
(page 206)

½ tsp. peppermint extract
green food coloring*

Mix on low speed until fully incorporated.

*Optional, depending on shell shape and desired look. I recommend leaving this out for candy cane macarons.

Swiss
MERINGUE

....

SWISS MERINGUE IS SIMILAR TO BUTTERCREAM in the sense that it is a great blank slate for various flavor profiles. The consistency is silky and wonderful. It is a thinner filling, so the shells have a tendency to slip and slide a little more than with buttercream. I usually make a large batch of Swiss meringue and stop right before adding any extracts and divide it up to make a multitude of flavors. Swiss meringue can be stored for up to ten days in your fridge. Just be sure to bring it up to room temperature before piping onto your macarons. Each Swiss Meringue recipe will make about three cups.

• VANILLA SWISS MERINGUE •

3 egg whites
¾ cup superfine sugar
simmering water

1 cup butter, softened and cut into
2-inch pieces
½ tsp. vanilla bean paste

In a heatproof bowl, lightly whisk egg whites and sugar over simmering water until the sugar fully dissolves (it feels smooth and not gritty when you rub it between your fingers) and the mixture is warm to the touch.

Remove mixture from the heat and whisk on low speed. Gradually increase speed until mixture doubles in volume into a meringue with stiff peaks.

On low speed, add butter one piece at a time.

Once all the butter is incorporated, replace whisk with paddle/beater attachment. Add vanilla bean paste and mix on medium speed for 3 minutes.

210

• CHOCOLATE SWISS MERINGUE •

3 egg whites
¾ cup superfine sugar
simmering water

1 cup butter, softened and cut into
   2-inch pieces
½ tsp. vanilla bean paste
1 Tbsp. cocoa powder
4 oz. melted chocolate*

Make basic vanilla Swiss meringue (page 210). Add in cocoa powder and mix to combine. Fold melted and cooled chocolate into meringue.

Milk, dark, white, or any other chocolate you prefer.

• COCONUT SWISS MERINGUE •

3 egg whites
¾ cup superfine sugar
simmering water
1 cup butter, softened and cut into
   2-inch pieces

½ tsp. vanilla bean paste
⅓ cup coconut milk
½ cup coconut flakes
½ cup powdered sugar

Make basic vanilla Swiss meringue (page 210). Add coconut milk, coconut flakes, and powdered sugar. Combine on medium-low speed for 3 minutes.

Gourmet French Macarons

Ganache

THESE RECIPES ARE FOR THE CHOCOLATE LOVERS OUT THERE! They are rich and have a wonderful, deep chocolate flavor. A basic ganache is made with two ingredients: chocolate and cream. The ratio will determine the texture and consistency. For macarons, we want a consistency that will easily pipe but not run over the side. There is great room for creativity here—adding flavorings is common. Just be sure to keep the same ratio of chocolate to liquid to maintain the proper texture. I recommend making and using the ganache on the same day, but it will keep in your fridge for a week. Be sure to bring it to room temperature before piping.

• MILK CHOCOLATE GANACHE •

3.5 oz. (100 g) milk chocolate*   1½ Tbsp. heavy cream

Place chocolate in a heatproof bowl. Boil cream and pour over chocolate. Stir until all the chocolate has melted and texture is smooth.** Let cool to room temperature before piping.

Use baking chocolate or chocolate chips. I prefer to use the mini chocolate chips when possible to speed up the process.

** *If the cream is not able to melt all the chocolate, place bowl in microwave. Heat for 20 seconds on low. Remove and stir. Repeat until chocolate is fully melted.*

• DARK CHOCOLATE GANACHE •

Substitute dark chocolate for milk chocolate in recipe above

• WHITE CHOCOLATE GANACHE •

Substitute white chocolate for milk chocolate in recipe above

Mindy Cone

Fruity
FILLINGS

Fruity FILLINGS

W HILE THESE FRUITY FLAVORS LEND THEMSELVES well to butter-
cream recipes, sometimes you want an extra punch of flavor. Most of these recipes
will produce a strong bite perfect for the center of a macaron. Often the consistency is thin, so I recommend using them in conjunction with other fillings. By piping a
dam around the edge of the macaron with another filling, you can place a dollop of the fruit
filling in the center and gently place the other shell on top—sealing the punch of flavor in the
middle. It is not only a wonderful surprise but also a great opportunity to combine flavors for
a complex taste.

• FRESH MACERATED BERRIES •

Strawberry, Raspberry, Blueberry, or Blackberry

2 cups coarsely cut fresh berries*   1 tsp. fresh lemon juice
2 Tbsp. superfine sugar

Combine ingredients and set aside to macerate for 30 minutes. Chop berries to desired
consistency and stir to combine with juices. Pipe another filling of choice around edge of macaron—I recommend a thicker filling (buttercream, ganache, or cream cheese). Then spoon
berry mixture into the center. Top with anther macaron shell to seal. Keep in fridge for up to
24 hours. (I enjoy them most after about 6 hours in the fridge).

Choose one or more berries as long as they combine for a total of 2 cups.

214

Mindy Cone

• APPLE COMPOTE •

1 cup water
2½ Tbsp. sugar
1 tsp. vanilla bean paste
¼ tsp. cinnamon

pinch nutmeg
pinch salt
4 peeled, cored apples,
   cut into ½-inch cubes

Combine water, sugar, vanilla bean paste, cinnamon, nutmeg, and salt in a medium saucepan. Bring to a boil. Reduce heat and simmer 5–10 minutes. Add apples and bring to a boil again. Reduce heat and simmer 10 minutes or until apples are tender but still hold their shape. Remove from heat and cool to room temperature. Place directly onto macaron shell or pipe desired filling* around edge of macaron and spoon apple compote in the center. Top with anther macaron shell to seal.

*I recommend cream cheese buttercream filling (page 208).

• HONEY-ROASTED PEAR COMPOTE •

2 ripe pears
1 Tbsp. butter
¼ cup apple juice

juice of 1 lemon
1 Tbsp. honey

Preheat oven to 375 degrees. Peel, halve, and pit pears. Butter bottom of 2-inch-deep oven-safe dish and place pears inside cut side down. Combine apple and lemon juice and pour over pears. Drizzle honey over top of pears. Place in oven for 45 minutes uncovered or until pears are soft all the way through. Remove from oven and allow to cool. Remove pear from juice and chop to small pieces. Place directly onto macaron shell or pipe another desired filling around edge of macaron and spoon pear compote in the center. Top with another macaron shell to seal.

• MANGO CURD •

½ cup sugar
¾ cup fresh pureed mango
2 Tbsp. fresh lime juice

pinch of salt
4 egg yolks
4 Tbsp. butter, room temperature

Combine sugar, mango, lime juice, salt, and egg yolks in blender or food processor and pulse until combined. Press through sieve to strain out any solids. Discard what is left in sieve, and place strained liquid into a metal bowl. Place bowl over simmering water, but do not allow the bottom of the bowl to touch the water. Whisk until mixture thickens and is hot to the touch (5–10 minutes). Remove from heat and allow to cool to lukewarm. Whisk in butter one tablespoon at a time. Place in an airtight container and refrigerate for 12 hours before use. Pipe directly onto macaron shell or pipe another desired filling around edge of macaron to create a dam and spoon mango curd into the center. Makes about 1 cup and will keep in refrigerator for up to 2 weeks.

• COCONUT CURD •

½ cup sugar
4 egg yolks
⅔ cup coconut milk
   (5½-oz. can)

pinch of salt
4 Tbsp. butter, room temperature

Whisk together sugar, egg yolks, coconut milk, and salt in a metal bowl. Place bowl over simmering water, making sure that the bottom of the bowl does not touch the water. Whisk until mixture thickens and is hot to the touch (5–10 minutes). Remove from heat and allow to cool to lukewarm. Whisk in butter one or two tablespoons at a time. Place in an airtight container and refrigerate for 12 hours before use. Pipe directly onto macaron shell or pipe another desired filling around edge of macaron to create a dam and spoon coconut curd into the center. Makes about 1 cup and will keep in refrigerator up to 2 weeks.

Mindy Cone

• LIME CURD •

½ cup sugar

zest of 3 limes

½ cup fresh lime juice

pinch of salt

4 egg yolks

4 Tbsp. butter, room temperature

Whisk together sugar, lime zest, lime juice, salt, and egg yolks in a metal bowl. Place bowl over simmering water, making sure that the bottom of the bowl does not touch the water. Whisk gently until mixture thickens and is hot to the touch (5–10 minutes). Remove from heat and allow to cool to lukewarm. Whisk in butter one or two tablespoons at a time. Place in an airtight container and refrigerate for 12 hours before use. Pipe directly onto macaron shell or pipe another desired filling around edge of macaron to create a dam and spoon lime curd into the center. Makes about 2 cups and will keep in refrigerator up to 2 weeks.

• LEMON CURD •

Substitute lemon zest and juice instead of lime in the lime curd recipe above.

• ORANGE CURD •

Substitute orange zest and juice instead of lime in the lime curd recipe above.

• PASSION FRUIT CURD •

Substitute ¾ cup passion fruit puree instead of mango in mango curd recipe (page 216).

• PEACH JAM •

5 peaches   1 Tbsp. lemon juice
1½ cups sugar   1 tsp. salt

Peel, pit, and cut peaches into ¼-inch pieces and toss with sugar, lemon juice, and salt in a large saucepan. Let stand for 3–4 hours at room temperature, re-tossing a few times throughout. Bring mixture to a boil over medium-high heat for about 20 minutes or until the liquid has a syrup texture and coats the back of a spoon. Keep in mind that the jam will thicken as it cools. Remove from heat and pour into container. Once cooled, the jam can be stored in the fridge for up to 1 month and in the freezer for up to 3 months. Makes about 1½ cups.

• APRICOT JAM •

Substitute 8–10 fresh apricots for the peaches in the peach jam recipe above.

• PLUM JAM •

Substitute 6–8 plums for the peaches in the peach jam recipe above.

• PINEAPPLE JAM •

1 pineapple   ½ cup water
1 cup sugar   3 Tbsp. lime juice

Peel, core, and grate fresh pineapple. Combine all ingredients in a saucepan. Simmer uncovered on low for 45–55 minutes or until thickened. Keep in mind that the jam will thicken as it cools. Remove from heat and pour into container. Once cooled, the jam can be stored in the fridge for up to 1 month and in the freezer for up to 3 months. Makes about 1½ cups.

Mindy Cone

• FIG JAM •

1 lb. mission figs (about 10)   ½ cup water
½ cup sugar   2 Tbsp. lemon juice

Remove stems of figs and chop into quarters. Combine ingredients in a saucepan and simmer uncovered on low for 45–55 minutes or until thickened. (Jam will continue to thicken as it cools.) Remove from heat and pour into container. Once cooled, the jam can be stored in the fridge for up to 1 month and in the freezer for up to 3 months. Makes about 1½ cups.

• CHERRY BUTTERCREAM •

½ cup frozen whole cherries,   1 tsp. cherry extract
   thawed, or fresh pitted cherries
2 cups vanilla bean buttercream
   (page 206)

Chop cherries and add to vanilla buttercream. Add cherry extract and mix on low speed until fully incorporated.

• WATERMELON BUTTERCREAM •

2 cups vanilla bean buttercream   1 tsp. watermelon oil
   (page 206)

Mix ingredients on low speed until fully incorporated.

• GRAPE BUTTERCREAM •

2 cups vanilla bean buttercream   ¾ cup grape jelly
   (page 206)

Mix ingredients on medium speed until fully incorporated.

Gourmet French Macarons

Seasonal
FILLINGS

Seasonal FILLINGS

M ACARONS LEND THEMSELVES BEAUTIFULLY to seasonal flavors. They are one of my favorites to make and share with friends during the holidays!

• ORANGE–CRANBERRY JAM •

1 orange—zest and juice
½ cup water
¾ cup sugar

pinch of salt
1 (12-oz.) bag fresh cranberries

Zest and juice one orange and add water, sugar, and salt in a medium saucepan. Bring to a boil and stir in cranberries. Reduce heat to low and simmer until sauce thickens and cranberries burst (10–12 minutes). (Jam will continue to thicken as it cools.) Allow to cool completely and spoon directly onto macaron shell.

• APPLE PIE •

1 cup apple compote (page 215)
1 cup cream cheese filling (page 208)

1 tsp. cinnamon

Combine ingredients on low speed and pipe onto macaron shell.

SHORTCUT: Buy an apple pie! I have scraped out the filling of a store-bought pie, chopped it into smaller pieces, and piped it onto macarons.

222

Mindy Cone

• PUMPKIN PIE •

2 eggs

1 (15-oz.) can pumpkin puree

½ cup sugar

¼ cup brown sugar

½ tsp. salt

½ tsp. ground cinnamon

½ tsp. ground nutmeg

½ tsp. ground cloves

½ tsp. ground ginger

1 (12-oz.) can evaporated milk

Preheat oven to 475 degrees and grease an 8-inch pie pan. Beat eggs in a large bowl. Add in pumpkin puree, sugar, brown sugar, salt, cinnamon, nutmeg, cloves, and ginger and beat on low speed. Once fully incorporated, slowly stir in evaporated milk. Pour filling into pie pan and bake for 15 minutes. Reduce temperature to 350 degrees and continue to cook for about 40 minutes or until center is set. Remove and allow to cool to room temperature. Pie filling can be placed directly into a pastry bag and piped onto macarons or combined with 2 cups of cream cheese filling (page 208) and piped onto the shells.

SHORTCUT: Buy a pumpkin pie! I have scraped out the filling of a store-bought pumpkin pie and piped it onto macarons.

• PECAN PIE •

1 cup whole pecans

2 eggs

1 cup light corn syrup

1 Tbsp. molasses

2 Tbsp. butter, melted

3 Tbsp. flour

pinch of salt

1 tsp. vanilla bean paste

Preheat oven to 375 degrees and grease 8-inch pie pan or 8 × 8 pan. Spread pecans across bottom of pan. Blend the remainder of ingredients and pour over the top of pecans. Bake for 35–45 minutes or until firm. Remove and allow to cool completely. Scrape off top layer of pecans and set aside. Place pie filling directly into a piping bag with a large circular tip and pipe onto macarons. Place whole pecan inside macaron and seal with more filling, or use to top as decoration.

223

• APPLE CIDER •

2 pkgs. instant apple cider mix
3 Tbsp. water

2 cups cream cheese buttercream filling (page 208)

Dissolve dry apple cider mix into water in a microwave-safe dish. Stir and place in microwave for 15 seconds. Repeat until mix is fully dissolved (it feels smooth and not gritty when you rub it between your fingers). Allow cider mixture to cool to room temperature and mix with cream cheese filling.

• MAPLE PECAN •

8 oz. cream cheese, room
    temperature
½ cup butter, room temperature
3½ cups powdered sugar

1 tsp. maple extract
¾ cup chopped pecans

Blend cream cheese and butter together. On low speed, add powdered sugar 1 cup at a time. Add maple extract and blend on high for 2–3 minutes. Stir in chopped pecans.

• EGGNOG •

8 oz. cream cheese, room
    temperature
½ cup butter, room temperature

4 cups powdered sugar
¼ cup eggnog
1 tsp. cinnamon

Blend cream cheese and butter together. On low speed, add powdered sugar 1 cup at a time. Add eggnog and cinnamon and blend on high for 2–3 minutes.

224

• WASSAIL BUTTERCREAM •

1 cup unsalted butter, softened
4½ cups sifted powdered sugar
1 tsp. cinnamon
1 tsp. ground cloves
1 tsp. nutmeg

1 tsp. vanilla bean extract
¼ cup orange marmalade
¼ cup pineapple marmalade
2 Tbsp. water
¼ tsp. salt

Mix butter and powdered sugar together on low speed. Add remaining ingredients and mix until smooth.

• SWEET POTATO •

4 oz. cream cheese, room
   temperature
¼ cup butter, room temperature
2½ cups powdered sugar
1 cup sweet potato puree

2 Tbsp. brown sugar
1 Tbsp. orange juice
1 tsp. cinnamon
¼ cup chopped pecans (optional)

Blend cream cheese and butter together. On low speed, add powdered sugar 1 cup at a time. Add remaining ingredients and mix until smooth.

I often fill my macarons with half sweet potato filling and half marshmallow filling to get that classic sweet potato casserole flavor!

225

• GINGERBREAD •

8 oz. cream cheese, room
temperature
½ cup butter, room temperature
3 cups powdered sugar
½ cup dark brown sugar

2 tsp. molasses
1 tsp. cinnamon
1 tsp. ginger
pinch of allspice
pinch of cloves

Blend cream cheese and butter together. On low speed, add powdered sugar 1 cup at a time. Add remaining ingredients and mix until smooth.

• CHOCOLATE CHIP BANANA BREAD •

4 oz. cream cheese, room
temperature
¼ cup butter, room temperature
1 large banana
½ tsp. lemon juice
2 cups powdered sugar

1 tsp. cinnamon
1 tsp. nutmeg
1 tsp. vanilla bean extract
¼ cup chopped chocolate chips or
mini chocolate chips

Beat cream cheese and butter together in a large bowl. In a small bowl, mash banana (should be about ½ cup) and add lemon juice to keep it from browning. Combine banana mixture and remaining ingredients, except chocolate chips, to cream cheese and butter mixture on low speed. Pipe filling onto macaron shell and sprinkle with mini chocolate chips. Top with similar-sized macaron shell.

Mindy Cone

• CANDY CORN BUTTERCREAM •

2 cups vanilla bean buttercream
  (page 206)
½ cup chopped candy corn

¾ cup whole candy corn
1 Tbsp. water

Mix vanilla buttercream and chopped candy corn together. Place the whole candy corn and water in a microwave-safe bowl. Microwave for 20 second intervals, stirring between each, until candy corn is melted. Set aside to cool to room temperature. Once cooled, mix melted candy corn into the buttercream.

• MINT CHOCOLATE GANACHE •

3.5 oz. (100 g) milk chocolate*
1 Tbsp. + 2 tsp. heavy cream

1 tsp. mint extract

Place chocolate in a heatproof bowl. Boil cream and pour over chocolate. Stir until all the chocolate has melted and texture is smooth.** Add mint extract and stir until smooth. Let cool to room temperature before piping.

*Use baking chocolate or chocolate chips. I prefer to use mini chocolate chips when possible to speed up the process.

**If the cream is not able to melt all the chocolate, place bowl in microwave. Heat for 20 seconds on low power. Remove and stir. Repeat until chocolate is fully melted.

227

• CINNAMON CHOCOLATE GANACHE •

3.5 oz. (100 g) milk chocolate*   1 tsp. cinnamon
1½ Tbsp. heavy cream

Place chocolate in a heatproof bowl. Boil cream and cinnamon and pour over chocolate. Stir until all the chocolate has melted and texture is smooth.** Let cool to room temperature before piping.

*Use baking chocolate or chocolate chips. I prefer to use the mini chocolate chips when possible to speed up the process.

**If the cream is not able to melt all the chocolate, place bowl in microwave. Heat for 20 seconds on low. Remove and stir. Repeat until chocolate is fully melted.

Mindy Cone

Candy Bar & Cookie
FILLINGS

Candy Bar
& COOKIE FILLINGS

 CLASSIC COMBINATIONS of flavors inspired by your favorite cookies and candy bars!

• MINT CHOCOLATE CHIP •

1 cup chocolate buttercream filling
(page 206)
1 cup mint buttercream filling
(page 209)

1 Tbsp. water
½ cup chopped chocolate chips
or mini chocolate chips

Pipe chocolate buttercream along the outside of the macaron shell to create a dam. Blend mint buttercream and water for 2–3 minutes on high. Sprinkle chopped chocolate chips inside of the chocolate buttercream in the center of the macaron shell. Fill remaining space in center with whipped mint buttercream and top gently with the other macaron shell, creating a seal with the chocolate buttercream.

• CHOCOLATE COCONUT JOY •

1 cup chocolate buttercream filling
(page 206)

½ cup finely chopped almonds
1 cup coconut Swiss meringue
filling (page 211)

Pipe chocolate buttercream along the outside of the macaron shell to create a dam. Sprinkle chopped almonds inside of the chocolate buttercream in the center of the macaron shell. Fill remaining space in center with coconut Swiss meringue and top gently with the other macaron shell, creating a seal with the chocolate buttercream.

Mindy Cone

• S'MORE •

1 cup chocolate buttercream filling
(page 206)
½ cup coarsely crushed graham
cracker

1 cup marshmallow filling
(page 238)

Pipe chocolate buttercream along the outside of the macaron shell to create a dam. Sprinkle graham cracker crumbs inside of the chocolate buttercream in the center of the macaron shell. Fill remaining space in center with marshmallow filling and top gently with the other macaron shell, creating a seal with the chocolate buttercream.

• SNICKERS •

1 cup chocolate buttercream filling
(page 206)
½ cup finely chopped peanuts

1 cup salted caramel sauce
(page 237)*

Pipe chocolate buttercream along the outside of the macaron shell to create a dam. Sprinkle chopped peanuts inside of the chocolate buttercream in the center of the macaron shell. Fill remaining space in center with salted caramel sauce and top gently with the other macaron shell, creating a seal with the chocolate buttercream.

*You can use a store-bought caramel sauce if needed.

• COOKIES 'N CREAM •

1 cup vanilla buttercream (page
206) or cream cheese buttercream (page 208)

6 chocolate sandwich cookies

Smash cookies as fine as possible and combine with filling of choice.

Gourmet French Macarons

• COOKIE DOUGH •

½ cup butter
¼ cup brown sugar
1 Tbsp. sugar
½ cup powdered sugar
½ cup flour

pinch of salt
1 Tbsp. almond milk*
1 tsp. vanilla bean extract
¼ cup chopped chocolate chips or mini chocolate chips

Cream butter, brown sugar, and sugar together. Add remaining ingredients one at a time and mix until combined.

Plain milk will work as well. Just be sure to keep the filling refrigerated until consuming.

• TOFFEE BAR CRUNCH •

2 cups chocolate buttercream (page 206) or dark chocolate ganache (page 212)

¾ cup salted caramel sauce (page 237)**
¾ cup toffee bits

Pipe chocolate filling along the outside of the macaron shell to create a dam. Sprinkle toffee bits inside of the chocolate filling in the center of the macaron shell. Fill remaining space in center with salted caramel sauce and top gently with the other macaron shell, creating a seal with the chocolate buttercream.

**You can substitute a store-bought caramel sauce if needed.*

Mindy Cone

• SNICKERDOODLE •

1 cup cream cheese buttercream
   filling (page 208)
1½ tsp. cinnamon

1 Tbsp. brown sugar

Mix ingredients on low speed until fully incorporated.

I usually dust the top of the macaron shell with cinnamon sugar to give it added snickerdoodle texture!

• PEANUT BUTTER CUP •

1 cup chocolate buttercream (page
   206) or dark chocolate ganache
   (page 212)
½ cup chopped peanut butter
cups

1 cup peanut butter*

Pipe chocolate filling along the outside of the macaron shell to create a dam. Sprinkle chopped peanut butter cups inside of the chocolate filling in the center of the macaron shell. Fill remaining space in center with peanut butter and top gently with the other macaron shell, creating a seal with the chocolate buttercream.

*You can substitute this with peanut butter whipped buttercream (page 207).

233

Gourmet French Macarons

More Flavors
& COMBINATIONS

FLAVORS & *More* COMBINATIONS

T HE POSSIBILITIES ARE ENDLESS! Here are some flavors and combinations that I love.

• CAKE BATTER BUTTERCREAM •

1 cup unsalted butter, softened
3 cups sifted powdered sugar
½ cup boxed cake mix*
1½ tsp. vanilla bean paste

1 tsp. almond extract
2 Tbsp. water
¼ tsp. salt

Mix butter, powdered sugar, and cake mix together on low speed. Add vanilla bean paste, almond extract, water, and salt. Mix on high speed until smooth.

You can substitute this with peanut butter whipped buttercream (page 207).

• CARROT CAKE •

1 cup cream cheese buttercream
   filling (page 208)
1 tsp. cinnamon

pinch nutmeg
½ cup grated carrots
½ cup powdered sugar

Mix all ingredients together on low speed until full incorporated.

Mindy Cone

• SALTED CARAMEL SAUCE •

½ cup heavy cream
1 tsp. vanilla bean paste
1¼ cup sugar
1 Tbsp. water
¼ tsp. salt

1 Tbsp. light corn syrup
4 Tbsp. unsalted butter, at room
    temperature, cut into 1-inch
    pieces

Heat cream and vanilla bean paste in a small saucepan over medium-high heat and bring to just under a boil, stirring occasionally, and then reduce heat to low. In a medium saucepan combine sugar, water, salt, and corn syrup. Bring to a boil over medium heat, stirring to dissolve the sugar. Continue to cook without stirring for 5–8 minutes or until the mixture is amber color. Then remove from the heat. Watch closely since it can burn quickly. Slowly add the cream to the sugar syrup. Use caution since the caramel will boil furiously at first and increase greatly in volume. Once the mixture simmers down, whisk until smooth and let it cool for about 10 minutes. Add butter pieces to the caramel one at a time, whisking after each addition until caramel is cool.

• ORANGE CREAMSICLE •

2 cups cream cheese buttercream
    filling (page 208), divided
½ tsp. orange extract

½ tsp. orange zest
orange food coloring

Fill piping bag with 1 cup cream cheese filling. Separately, blend the remaining vanilla cream cheese filling, orange extract, and orange zest. Add orange food coloring to reach desired color. Fill a second piping bag with this mixture. Pipe white cream cheese filling along the outside of the macaron shell to create a dam. Fill remaining space in center with orange filling and top gently with the other macaron shell, creating a seal with the cream cheese filling

237

Gourmet French Macarons

• MARSHMALLOW •

4 egg whites
1 cup sugar
½ cup light corn syrup

4 Tbsp. water
1 Tbsp. vanilla bean extract
pinch of salt

Combine all ingredients in a large metal bowl. Place bowl over simmering water but do not allow the bottom of the bowl to touch the water. Beat on high speed for about 10 minutes or until mixture thickens and doubles. Remove from heat and continue to beat as mixture cools to lukewarm.

• HONEY BUTTERCREAM •

2 cups vanilla bean buttercream
   filling (page 206)

¼ cup honey

Mix ingredients on low speed until fully incorporated. Pipe the honey buttercream along the outside of the macaron shell to create a dam. Then, fill remaining space in center with additional honey and top gently with the other macaron shell, creating a seal with the buttercream. This will give you an extra honey bite in the center!

• PEANUT BUTTER & JELLY •

1 cup peanut butter whipped
   buttercream (page 207)

¼ cup jelly

Pipe peanut butter whipped buttercream along the outside of the macaron shell to create a dam. Place a dollop of jelly in the center and top gently with the other macaron shell, creating a seal with the buttercream.

Mindy Cone

• BANANA CREAM PIE •

1 pkg. instant banana pie pudding
1 banana

2 cups marshmallow filling
(page 238)

Make pudding according to package directions but reduce the liquid to ¾ the suggested amount. Place in fridge and allow to set up. Cut banana into thin slices. Pipe a small amount of banana pudding onto your macaron shell and top with a banana slice. Then pipe a small amount of marshmallow filling on top of the banana and seal with second macaron shell.

This filling will not keep as long in the refrigerator. Serve within 2 days to ensure proper texture.

• DULCE DE LECHE •

1 (14-oz.) can of sweetened
   condensed milk*

1 cup vanilla bean buttercream
   (page 206) or cream cheese
   buttercream (page 208)

Remove the label from the can of sweetened condensed milk and pierce 2–3 holes in the top of the can. Place in saucepan and fill with water to about ¾ the way up the can. Bring water to a simmer and cook for 3–4 hours uncovered. Replenish the water every 30 minutes. Remove can and allow to cool to room temperature. Open can and remove dulce de leche sauce. Combine buttercream and ½ cup of dulce de leche. Pipe this mixture along the outside of the macaron shell to create a dam. Place a dollop of dulce de leche inside of the buttercream in the center of the macaron shell and top gently with the other macaron shell, creating a seal with the buttercream.

*SHORTCUT: Use store-bought dulce de leche.

Gourmet French Macarons

• PIÑA COLADA •

¼ cup crushed
pineapple

1 cup coconut Swiss meringue
(page 211)

Drain and pat dry crushed pineapple. Measure ¼ cup and combine with meringue.

• THE ELVIS: PEANUT BUTTER BANANA •

1 cup peanut butter whipped
buttercream (page 207)

1 banana, sliced

Pipe a small amount of buttercream onto your macaron shell and top with a banana slice.
Pipe additional buttercream on top of the banana and seal with second macaron shell.

This filling will not keep long in the refrigerator. Serve within 2 days to ensure proper texture, or just eat it right away like I do. This is one of my favorites!

• CHOCOLATE PEANUT BUTTER BANANA •

1 cup peanut butter whipped
buttercream (page 207)
1 banana, sliced

1 cup chocolate buttercream
(page 206) or milk chocolate
ganache (page 212)

Pipe a small amount of peanut butter buttercream onto your macaron shell and top with a
banana slice. Pipe chocolate buttercream on top of the banana and seal with second macaron
shell.

This filling will not keep long in the refrigerator. Serve within 2 days to ensure proper texture. I also recommend using a larger macaron shell, 1½–2 inches.

Mindy Cone

• DARK CHOCOLATE POMEGRANATE •

2 cups pomegranate juice
1 cup butter, room temperature
4 cups sifted powder sugar

1 cup dark chocolate ganache
   (page 212)
1 fresh pomegranate (optional)

Place pomegranate juice into a saucepan and simmer on low uncovered until reduced and condensed to ½ cup. Cream butter and sugar together. Add cooled and reduced pomegranate juice and blend until fully incorporated. Pipe chocolate ganache along the outside of the macaron shell to create a dam. Fill remaining space in center with pomegranate buttercream. For added texture, cut open a fresh pomegranate and remove seeds. Press fresh pomegranate seeds gently into the buttercream and top with the other macaron shell, creating a seal with the chocolate ganache.

• MAPLE BROWN SUGAR & BACON •

4 slices thick-cut bacon
½ cup brown sugar, divided
1 cup cream cheese buttercream
   filling (page 208)

2 tsp. maple syrup
1 Tbsp. powdered sugar

Prepare baking sheet lined with foil and topped with a cooling rack or slotted roasting pan. Rub bacon generously with ¼ cup brown sugar and place on rack. Bake 20–25 minutes until extra crispy. Allow to cool, crumble bacon, and set aside. Combine ¼ cup brown sugar, cream cheese filling, maple syrup, and powdered sugar. Pipe filling mixture onto macaron shell. Press crumbled bacon generously (and gently) into the filling and top with the other macaron shell to create a seal.

Gourmet French Macarons

• WHITE CHOCOLATE & CARAMEL MACADAMIA NUT •

1 cup white chocolate ganache
(page 212)

½ cup caramel sauce (page 237)
¼ cup chopped macadamia
nuts

Pipe white chocolate ganache along the outside of the macaron shell to create a dam. Sprinkle chopped macadamia nuts inside of the chocolate buttercream in the center of the macaron shell. Fill remaining space in center with caramel sauce and top gently with the other macaron shell, creating a seal with the white chocolate buttercream.

• CHOCOLATE–COVERED CHERRY •

1 cup chocolate buttercream
(page 206)
½ cup frozen or fresh pitted and
chopped cherries

1 cup cherry buttercream
(page 219)

Pipe chocolate buttercream along the outside of the macaron shell to create a dam. Sprinkle chopped cherries inside of the chocolate buttercream in the center of the macaron shell. Fill remaining space in center with cherry buttercream and top gently with the other macaron shell, creating a seal with the chocolate buttercream.

• ROOT BEER SWISS MERINGUE •

3 egg whites
¾ cup superfine sugar

1¼ cup butter, softened and cut
into 2-inch pieces
½ tsp. root beer extract

In a heatproof bowl, lightly whisk egg whites and sugar over simmering water until the sugar fully dissolves (it feels smooth and not gritty when you rub it between your fingers) and the mixture is warm to the touch. Remove mixture from the heat and whisk on low speed. Gradually increase speed until mixture doubles in volume into a meringue with stiff peaks. Replace whisk with paddle/beater attachment. Add butter one piece at a time on low speed. Once all the butter is incorporated, add root beer extract and mix on medium speed for 3 minutes.

242

Mindy Cone

• PINK LEMONADE BUTTERCREAM •

3 Tbsp. pink lemonade powder
2 Tbsp. water
1 cup unsalted butter, softened

3½ cups sifted powdered sugar
¼ tsp. salt
zest of 1 lemon

Mix lemonade powder and water. Stir to dissolve. Separately, mix butter and powdered sugar together on low speed. Add salt, lemon zest, and lemonade powder mixture. Mix on high until smooth.

• CHOCOLATE MALT BUTTERCREAM •

¼ cup malted milk powder
5 Tbsp. water, divided
1 cup unsalted butter, softened
3½ cups sifted powdered sugar

1 cup cocoa powder
1½ tsp. almond extract
¼ tsp. salt
½ cup finely chopped malt balls
(optional)

Combine malted milk powder and 3 tablespoons water. Stir until completely dissolved. Mix butter and powdered sugar together on low speed. Add cocoa powder and continue to mix on low speed. Add almond extract, remaining water, and salt. Mix on high speed until smooth. For added texture, add chopped malt balls and incorporate on low speed.

• BUTTERSCOTCH BUTTERCREAM •

1 cup unsalted butter, softened
3½ cups sifted powdered sugar
1½ tsp. vanilla bean paste

1 tsp. almond extract
¼ tsp. salt
½ cup butterscotch sauce

Mix butter and powdered sugar together on low speed. Add vanilla bean paste, almond extract, salt, and butterscotch sauce. Mix on high speed until smooth.

243

Gourmet French Macarons

Store-Bought
IDEAS

Store-Bought IDEAS

M AYBE YOU JUST SPENT THE DAY MAKING MACARONS, and you don't feel like making a filling from scratch. Have no fear! Store-bought substitutes work great! Here is a list of shortcut options—just place a dollop between two shells and you are good to go!

- *Jellies, jams, preserves, and marmalades*—My favorites are raspberry jam, grape jelly, orange marmalade, and pineapple marmalade.

- *Sandwich spreads*—Peanut butter, almond butter, marshmallow fluff, and, of course, chocolate hazelnut spread!

- *Curd*—Lemon, lime, mango, and coconut curds are all great options. They can be a bit expensive, so I prefer to make my own when possible.

- *Fresh fruit*—Chopped or sliced thin.

- *Ice cream toppings*—In the store, these are in a great place to look for possible fillings! I often use these as a shortcut for caramel and butterscotch sauces.

Mindy Cone

- *Canned foods*—Cranberry sauce, crushed pineapple, and pie or pastry fillings make for great shortcuts.

- *Premade pies*—This may sound strange, but most premade pies can be scraped out and piped right on macarons! There is no better filling for a pumpkin macaron than real pumpkin pie! Again, I always prefer homemade, but in a pinch, it works great.

- *Ice cream*—One of my favorite treats is a macaron ice cream sandwich!

Gourmet French Macarons

Tips &
TROUBLESHOOTING

Tips &
TROUBLESHOOTING

MACARONS HAVE A REPUTATION FOR BEING TRICKY! These are some of the common questions and concerns I am asked about. With time, you will be a master at making classic and unique macarons!

Meringue won't stiffen	Not whipped long enough, bowl was not fully cleaned, trace of egg yolks, using fresh or cold egg whites, too much liquid dye added too early.
Almonds have skin on them	This will only affect appearance—they will cook the same but will have dark flecks in the shell.
Macaron shells have a grainy, rough texture	Undermixed, almond meal is not fine enough. Use a finer sieve.

250

Macaron shells have bubbles	Need to rap the sheet pan, pop bubbles with toothpick in early resting period, press batter against the edge of bowl when folding.
Macaron shells have peaks	Need to rap the sheet pan, place a warm sheet pan underneath and rap again, macaron batter is too thick and undermixed.
Macaron shells are not circular	Overmixed batter; uneven, warped, lopsided sheet pans; uneven parchment paper; piping at an angle. Use level sheet pans and secure parchment with magnets.
No feet	Undermixed, not resting long enough or resting too long, cooking at too low temperature.
Lopsided feet	Uneven, warped, or lopsided sheet pans; piping batter at an angle; piping batter too thin in areas or around edges; poor quality parchment.

251

Gourmet French Macarons

Protruding feet	Overmixed batter, under-whipped meringue, baking temperature too high.
Shrinking or "falling" feet	Normal to a certain extent—foot should remain, but it may get smaller or less pronounced when cooling.
Cracking	Oven too hot, need more resting time, dragged piping tip, or batter is too thin in area.
Sticking to parchment	Undercooked or overcooked, oven too hot or too cool, baked on poor-quality parchment, not cool enough to remove yet. If your macarons are undercooked, place them back in the oven for another minute or so and then repeat the cooling process. If they still stick, place them in the freezer for a few minutes once cooled and they should come right off. Some suggest adding hot water under the parchment paper to steam them free. I have had trouble with this method and do not recommend it.

Mindy Cone

Hollow	Undercooked, overmixed, too many air bubbles, or oven temperature too high. Press batter against the side of your bowl after each fold to remove air from batter. Drop oven temperature by 25 degrees and add 4 minutes baking time.
Browning	Cooked too long, oven temperature too high. Move rack away from oven heat source. Crack oven toward the end of cooking if they begin to brown and turn down temperature 25 degrees.
Wrinkled shells	Undercooked, overmixed, too many air bubbles
Overcooked	Fill and chill in the refrigerator an extra day—they will still be great, you just have to wait for them to mature a little longer.
Did you make a "bad" batch? Don't waste it!	Crumble them over ice cream or dessert bars! Drizzle chocolate over those ugly shells and top with a dollop of whipped cream—it's amazing! Mix them into chocolates or brownies! There are lots of ways to enjoy them!

253

Gourmet French Macarons

Acknowledgments

THIS BOOK HAS BEEN A DREAM COME TRUE, and I have been overwhelmed by the love and support from family, friends, and acquaintances! I could never express my gratitude adequately or show the magnitude of how much it means to me. You believed in me, cheered me on, gave advice, shared my work, and gave endless praise. It is because of you that this seedling of an idea has blossomed into this book.

I am so very thankful for my family! Randall, my love, you may have looked at me like I was crazy when I first told you I wanted to write a book—but from that second on, you never wavered in your love and support through the process. With all that you have going on at work, I'm not sure I could have picked a more challenging time to reach for this goal, but you still found ways to help, support, and encourage me so that I was able to achieve it. You are my best friend and the love of my life. Thank you for your love and belief in me and all my crazy dreams and ideas. My sweet children, Aubrey and Patton, thank you for your love. Although you are too young to remember this time clearly, you were incredibly loving and patient with all of my cookie making—even though you couldn't eat them..You are the reason I am inspired to be a more creative, imaginative, and hardworking mommy. I love you guys so much!

Mom and Dad, you taught me the value of being creative, dreaming big, and working hard to achieve it—among many other things. You live these principles. Thank you for your example. Your endless stream of support and praise kept me going when I needed it most. I could never have accomplished this without you. Dad, your example has taught me to work hard for my dreams, to not sweat the small things, and to never give up. Mom, there is no doubt that your creativity and craftiness and your love of entertaining and photography have inspired who I am today. To my siblings—Mandy, Ryan, and Taylor—you have been my biggest cheerleaders. From the start you believed in my idea and you believed in me. You have shared with your friends and solicited fans everywhere you went. Thank you, Mandy, for all of your advice and counsel. Taylor, you gave me the initial courage I needed—without this push, I would not have taken those critical first steps. To my wonderful extended family—thank you for your sweet words and loving messages of encouragement and praise. Thank you to the Cone family for your thoughtfulness and support during this process. I have felt your love many times through your caring gestures. I have been so blessed to have married into such a wonderful second family. In the beginning of this process, I was asked to come up with a marketing plan . . . I simply put "my family"—and it's true! You are my biggest supporters. Thank you for your love, encouragement, praise, and endless belief in me.

I have the most amazing friends. Where do I even begin? You were not only there to encourage me but also to relieve burdens. Thank you to all of you who saw a need and offered to watch my kids, bring me a meal, write a sweet note, and help in so many other ways. Thank you to my friends here and all over for your kind words, supportive attitude, and encouraging gestures—I have been overwhelmed by your thoughtfulness. A special thanks to Amanda of Traylor Made Treats—you were on speed dial for advice. Your friendship and willingness to help and encourage me has been amazing. You are incredibly talented, and I have been honored to work with you on so many occasions. Thank you also to my dear friend Kristy of Kristy G. Photography. Your wealth of photography advice and editing tips was so generously given at the most critical time during this process. Thank you for the beautiful headshot, all of your help, your encouragement, and, of course, your friendship. I could never have finished this book without my friends—thank you!

I have been blessed to meet and connect with so many talented and creative people through Creative Juice—many of whom have become great friends. I could never have imagined when I began this journey the magnitude of your support, generosity, and outpouring of love. With each milestone, you have been there to support and encourage. I am honored to be a part of such an incredible network of creative genius. It has been an amazing journey watching so many of you reach your dreams—thank you for being by my side as I have achieved one of mine!

Of course I want to say thank you to all of the supportive and amazing fans of Creative Juice! Whether you follow along through Facebook, Twitter, or Instagram, or if you subscribe to

Mindy Cone

the blog, it is because of YOU that I am able to achieve this dream. Your comments make my day. Your emails bring me huge smiles. Your encouraging words and thoughtful sentiments have connected us on so many occasions—and I am so thankful for you.

I would be just a girl with an idea had it not been for the incredible team at Cedar Fort Publishing. Thank you for believing in me, for understanding my vision, and for bringing something from my dreams into reality. You have given me so much advice and been so patient as I learned the ropes as a new author. Thank you Joanna Barker, Chloe Curtis, Erica Dixon, Casey Winters, and the entire Cedar Fort team for all you have done!

Index

259

260

Index

261

Index

About
the Author

© Kristy G. Photography

Mindy Cone is an entertainment, food, and party stylist on the popular blog Creative Juice. She writes about everything you need to know to entertain your guests and kids with style and creativity. Her love for macarons and perfectly themed parties inspired her to break from tradition and create macarons of different shapes for all occasions. Although an East Coast girl at heart, she currently lives in Northern California with her husband and two young children.

Visit Mindy's blog, Creative Juice, at www.getcreativejuice.blogspot.com

Praise for *Gourmet French Macarons*

"Prepare to be wowed! *Gourmet French Macarons* is absolutely fabulous! Whether you're an expert baker or just a beginner, you will learn how to make the most adorable *and* delectable macarons. A must-have book for all!"

—*Kara Allen*, author of *Kara's Party Ideas*

"As if macarons weren't cute enough, Mindy Cone has taken them into the cuteness stratosphere!"

—*Bridget Edwards*, author of *Decorating Cookies: 60+ Designs for Holidays, Celebrations & Everyday*

"Macarons are one of the hottest dessert trends on the table right now. From hamburgers to hearts, this book is filled to the brim with creative ways to tailor macarons to any theme."

—*Melissa Johnson*, BestFriendsforFrosting.com

"Macarons are an essential element to every dessert table! Mindy Cone provides a fresh twist on a classic cookie."

—*Kim Stoegbauer*, TheTomKatStudio.com

"This is a must-have book for all sweet treat lovers. The ideas and creative inspiration are perfect for everything from holidays to weddings to birthdays! *Gourmet French Macarons* will have a permanent place in my kitchen!"

—*Courtney Whitmore*, cookbook author and creator of Pizzazzerie.com

0 26575 12197 1

DINOFOURS

I'M THE BOSS!